America Zen

A Gathering of Poets

Edited with Introduction
by
Ray McNiece & Larry Smith

Harmony Series
Bottom Dog Press
Huron, Ohio

Bottom Dog Press, Inc.
PO Box 425
Huron, OH 44839
Lsmithdog@aol.com
Homepage:
http://members.aol.com/Lsmithdog/bottomdog

Credits
Cover art "12 Poems of Cold Mountain"
by George Fitzpatrick
Enso drawing by Lois Eby
Book layout and design by Larry Smith

Acknowledgments
We thank all the poets and publishers for allowing us
to print and reprint poems here.
In addition some specific poems are noted on page 220.

Our thanks for the continuing support of
The Ohio Arts Council

Ohio Arts Council
A STATE AGENCY
THAT SUPPORTS PUBLIC
PROGRAMS IN THE ARTS

Contents

From "Axe Handles"

It's in Lu Ji's *Wen Fu*, fourth century
A.D. "Essay on Literature"—in the
Preface: "In making the handle
Of an axe
By cutting wood with an axe
The model is indeed near at hand."
My teacher Shih-hsian Chen
Translated that and taught it years ago.
And I see: Pound was an axe,
Chen was an axe, I am an axe
And my son a handle, soon
To be shaping again, model
And tool, craft of culture,
How we go on.

Gary Snyder

Outside the Box, Inside the Circle
Introduction—Part One by Larry Smith

Who says my writing is poetry?
These poems are not poetry.
When you can understand this,
then we can speak of poetry.
        -Taigu Ryokan

To what shall I liken the world?
Moonlight, reflected in dewdrops
shaken from a crane's bill.
        -Dogen Zenji

The Rise of Zen Buddhism

In gathering this loose *sangha* of contemporary American poets, we discovered much about the nature of Zen Buddhist art and its impact on America and its poetry. Some of which we'll share here; much of which you will discover for yourself in your reading of these poems and personal Zen statements. Three main streams of the Zen outlook and aesthetic flow into the river of American poetry: the teachings and practice of Buddhism in America, the writings of older American Zen poets, and the translations of ancient Zen Buddhist writings into English, typically by modern and contemporary poets.

Always remarkable is the long history of this Buddhist influence, drawing upon a tradition that goes back 2,500 years to Shakyamuni Buddha's long journey and awakening under a bodhi tree. It then was spread throughout India and into Tibet as Vajrayana Buddhism, and was carried over the mountains to China by Bodhidharma around 500 AD, where its Mahayana branch merged with Taoism and Confucianism evolving into Chinese Ch'an and then Japanese Zen Buddhism. In Japanese monasteries two Zen schools emerged as Soto (just sitting) and Rinzai (training through koans and interviews). During China's Golden Ages of the T'ang (7th and 8th centuries) and Sung dynasties (10th-12th centuries) Zen flowered and spread through East Asia into such territories as Korea, Vietnam, and Cambodia. During the course of this evolution of Buddhism the mysticism of India was transformed by the utilitarian practice of Taoism and the communal wisdom of Confucianism. In the temples of China all three were practiced side by side bringing about a rich cross-fertilization.

In Zen practice almost exclusively the arts emerged as a tool for instruction in the Way, often taught by poet-priests. Thus the Buddhist arts of painting, gardening, flower arranging, calligraphy, the tea ceremony, body movement, shakahachi flute, Noh drama, and poetry evolved. As John Daido Loori points out in his *The Zen of Creativity* (Ballantine 2004), in this experiential religion and outlook these arts were created "to communicate the essential 'wordlessness' of Zen"(5). And so early Zen poetry took these forms: 1) The enlightenment poem, expressing the ineffable sense of awakening and presence, as a way to convey a Zen student's progress, 2) The death poem as a kind of legacy statement by Zen monks, expressing their sense of leaving yet non-leaving, 3) The offering poem expressing compassion and deep appreciation, 4) The liturgy poem used by Zen priests as 'dharma words' in instruction, 5) The koan (Zen puzzle) poem or story given for self-meditation, and accompanied by commentary or capping poems as pointers for the koan. Key among the Zen masters who developed Zen arts from Japan were Dogen Zenji (1200-1253), who first brought Soto Zen to Japan, Ikkyu (1394-1481), Hakuin Ekaku (1685-1768), and Taigu Ryokan (1758-1831). Each had a true, rebellious spirit and each wrote a spontaneous and intuitive poetry that treated reality directly using images to transcend a subject-object dualism. Dogen's *Shobogenzo*, serves as a poetic book of instruction and a work of art: "Because the blue mountains are walking, they are constant. Their walk is swifter than the wind. Yet those on the mountains do not sense this, do not know it." Symbol and reality are made one here. In other verse, Dogen uses language to offer a pointer, "To study the Way is to study the self./ To study the self is to forget the self./ To forget the self is to be enlightened by the ten thousand things [reality]" or "Seeing form with the whole body and mind,/ Hearing sound with the whole body and mind,/ One understands It intimately"(quoted in Loori 45, 49, 67). In America, Dogen Zenji has become the pervasive influence on Zen Buddhist practice and art.

Zen Buddhism in America

Just as Zen Buddhism evolved through its early migration in the Far East, so its movement to America is a revealing story. And it has been best told by Rick Fields' *How the Swans Came to the Lake: A Narrative History of Buddhism in America* (Shambhala 1981; rev. 1992).* A brief summary of the major Zen Buddhist migration to and across America can be helpful. While the American Transcendentalists published the first "Introduction to Buddhism" in Elizabeth Peabody's translation for *Dial* magazine in 1844, America did not have a real Zen teacher until D. T. Suzuki (1870-1966), a Japanese scholar and Zen practitioner, arrived at Columbia University in 1896. He came to teach world religions and collaborte on an English translation of the *Tao te Ching*. For decades he wrote and lectured around the country, producing our earliest translations of Buddhist works and serving as our primary 'translator' of Zen thought through a series of *Essays in Zen Buddhism* launched in 1927 (London). His *An Introduction* *to Zen Buddhism* published in 1949 was given a foreword by C. G. Jung (London, The Buddhist Society). Suzuki later befriended most of the Zen teachers and translators who came to America, including Shunryu Suzuki and Alan Watts, an Anglican priest. Watts, who migrated to America in 1938, became a chief interpreter of Eastern religions to the West through his countless talks and books. In particular his *The Way of Zen* (NY: New American Library 1957) did much to popularize Zen study and practice. Later his *Beat Zen, Square Zen, and Zen* (SF: City Lights Books 1959) revealed the Zen spirit in the Beat Movement.

The wave of Japanese Zen Buddhist teachers came slowly at first. Zen poet Nyogen Senzaki (18??-1968), sometimes referred to as "the Bodhisattva of Buddhism to America" began teaching on the West Coast in 1905, later helping to translate Zen stories, poems, and koans with Ruth Strout McCandless and Paul Reps. Early teaching visits followed from Japanese Rinzai priests Soen Nakagawa (1907-1984) and Hakuun Yasutani (1885-1973). A much larger wave came with the moving to America of Taizan Maezumi (1931-1995) in 1956 and of Shunryu Suzuki (1904-1971) in 1959. Though each trained separately, they became allies in the transmigration of Zen Buddhism to the West. Maezumi Roshi came to Los Angeles as a priest at Zenshuji Temple, the Soto headquarters of the United States, and eventually established the Zen Center of Los Angeles in 1967, followed by centers in California's San Jacinto Mountains and in Mexico City. Suzuki began his service as a Zen master at San Francisco's Sojoki Temple and became first abbot of the San Francisco Zen Center, later developing the Tassajara Mountain Center and Green Gulch Farm. Both trained several American priests in their lineage and numerous American lay Buddhists at their centers and through their writings. Unique to the American setting was the integration of Rinzai (koan) and Soto (sitting) developed by these men, both of whom held Dogen Zenji as central to their teaching. In addition, they became allies with Chogyam Trungpa Rinpoche in his practice of Tibetan Buddhism. Trungpa had fled Tibet and come to American in the mid-1960's where he founded the first Buddhist university in America, the Naropa Institute of Boulder, Colorado, which merged with the Jack Kerouac School of Disembodied Poetics co-founded by poets Allen Ginsberg, Anne Waldman, and Diane di Prima. This cross-fertilization or 'impure' blending of Buddhist schools has became a characteristic of American Zen practice. Each of these Buddhist teachers has produced key books that have impacted the practice of Buddhism in America, to list only one: Suzuki's *Zen Mind, Beginner's Mind* (NY: Weatherhill 1970) edited by his student Trudy Dixon has gone through countless printings, making it the most popular book on Zen Buddhism in America. Maezumi's *On Zen Practice* (L.A.

Zen Center 1976, rpt. 2002) co-edited with his successor Bernard Glassman has been enlarged by his *Appreciate Your Life: The Essence of Zen Practice* (Shambhala 2001). Chogyam Trungpa's most popular book is *Shambhala: Sacred Path of the Warrior* (Shambhala 1984).

In coming to America, Zen has been transformed. Though American teachers in the lineage were at first sent back to Japan for additional training and approval, eventually, Suzuki and Maezumi each began passing their own stamp of approval on American Zen Buddhist successors, men and women. Maezumi Roshi founded the White Plum Sangha and has transmitted the Dharma to successors: Bernard Tetsugen Glassman, Dennis Genpo Merzel, Charlotte Joko Beck, Jan Chozen Bays, John Daido Loori, and others. Shunryu Suzuki's successors include Richard Baker, Reb Anderson, Japanese monk Dainin Katagiri who moved on to direct the Minnesota Zen Center, Mel Weitsman, Grahame Petchey, Norman Fischer, Blanche Hartman, and others. And these Zen masters have produced their own teachings in study centers and books and passed their *stupa* on to others. Many of the poets in this collection have worked with these mentors. Other important Buddhist teachers in America would include the frequent visits from the Dali Lama, Robert Aitken of the Diamond Sanga in Hawaii, Phillip Kapleau in Rochester's Zen Center, Pema Chodron of the Gampo Abbey in Nova Scotia, and Thich Nhat Hanh, with centers in Vietnam, France, and America. The Insight Mediation Group (Sharon Salzberg, Jack Kornfield, Joseph Goldstein, Larry Rosenberg, et al) are Tibetan trained but open to many forms of Buddhism and place a clear emphasis on applying *metta* or loving-kindness to psychology and social issues.

Characterizing the practice of American Zen Buddhism is difficult because it remains in transition, but a few things are clear: though no less sincere, it is less rigorous than its Japanese practice which is strong on tradition and endurance, and it is more open to cross-fertilization and broader in its appeal. As a religion it is not dogmatic or evangelical; as an outlook it is open, positive, and inclusive. Primarily American Zen is a lay practice, meant to be shared by many and incorporated into their daily lives outside of a monastery. Today it can be found in most metropolitan areas as well as in mountain and dessert retreats which remain available for weekend training in basic meditation and Zen arts or in month long *sesshin*. Meditation remains at the heart of this experiential training; poetry is seen as a natural expression of the original self. While large publishing houses do Buddhists writings regularly, certain American presses have a record of commitment to producing books on Buddhist practice and art, included among those are: Tuttle, Weatherhill, Wisdom, North Point, Shambhala, and Copper Canyon presses.

The Rise of American Zen Poetry

Before Dogen Zenji's influence would be felt in the mid-1960's when Japanese priests came to America, the voices of Zen came through the early translations of the pre-T'ang poets T'ao Ch'ien (365-427) and Hsieh Ling-Yun (385-433), T'ang poets Wang Wei (701-761), Li Po (701-762), Tu Fu (712-770), Han-Shan ('Cold Mountain' c. 7th-9th centuries), Po Chu-I (772-846), Chia Tao (779-843), Tu Mu (803-853), and the Sung Dynasty poets Su Tung-P'o (1037-1101), Lu Yu (1125-1210), and Yang Wan-Li (1127-1206). These works presented an intimate voice and outlook centered in concrete images within a sense of life's Oneness. This affected American thought and impacted modern poetry early on through the Imagist school of Ezra Pound, Amy Lowell, H. D., William Carlos Williams, Wallace Stevens, whose primary maxim became, "No ideas but in Things." The principles of Imagism as expressed in the "Imagist Manifesto" include the use of "the language of common speech . . . the exact word, not the nearly-exact, nor the merely decorative word," free verse cadences and freedom of subject matter with an emphasis on the concrete. Imagist poets shared these goals: "To present an image. We are not a school of painters, but we believe that poetry should render particulars exactly and not deal in vague generalities" and "To produce a poetry that is hard and clear, never blurred and indefinite." Ultimately they declared *concentration* as "the very essence of poetry." Recall that these poets were breaking from the rigidity of 19th century formalism and a lofty romanticism. Though Emerson, Thoreau, and Walt Whitman were calling for a new concreteness, the predominant 19th century poetic voices were still Henry Wadsworth Longfellow, John Greenleaf Whittier, even Edgar Allen Poe.

During the early modernist period, we witness a natural American Zen poetry expressing a spontaneous and intuitive sense of being. Wallace Stevens' "Thirteen Ways of Looking at a Blackbird" (1917) fits well here, "I was of three minds,/ Like a tree/ In which there are three blackbirds" or William Carlos Williams' glistening red wheelbarrow beside the white chickens, a concrete Zen koan still (1923). But perhaps most in the Zen aesthetic is the contemplative "Ars Poetica" of Archibald MacLeish (1926) which expresses and reveals a poetry of essences. "A poem should be palpable and mute/ as a globed fruit . . ." he declares, then using images to speak, takes us through the very process of a poem's inner movement to its ultimate realization, "A poem should not mean/ but be." This experiential basis for art makes perfect Zen-sense, anywhere, any time.

For the poets gathered here there is also the work of fellow Zen poets, American and in translation. The immediate predecessor to this collection came from Shambhala Publications in 1991, eclectically grouped under its title, *Beneath a Single Moon*. Editors Craig Paulenich and Kent

Johnson found many paths toward the Oneness of awakened experience and "a tradition of poetic stance that bears marked affinities with Buddhist principles and the identity of subject and object, meaning and form" (*Beneath* xvii). Many of the poets assembled there are gathered here as well; thus Sam Hamill, Jane Hirshfield, William Heyen, Diane di Prima, Anne Waldman, Margaret Gibson, Andrew Schelling, and I are represented in more recent work here. Our contemporary focus has gathered a younger and more diverse group of poets. Thus, fine American Zen poets Gary Snyder, Philip Whalen, Lucien Stryk, Allen Ginsberg, Norman Fischer, Joanne Kyger, and Jim Harrison do not appear, though their influence is clearly represented and perhaps pervasive. Jack Kerouac's Beat Zen haiku have had a large impact on many young writers. Our goal here was to produce a vital collection of American Buddhist writing, not to make *the* American Zen Buddhist poetry anthology. Drawing the circle wider than our limited 30 poets, we have included a listing of most of the 200 poets who offered their fine work to us as American Zen poets. Other fine American poets affected by Zen would include James Wright, W. S. Merwin, Mary Oliver.

Gary Snyder's clear introduction to *Beneath a Single Moon* places a strong emphasis on meditation practice as the poet's writing source and guide: "Meditation is not just a rest or retreat form the turmoil of the stream or the impurity of the world. It is a way of being the stream . . . . Meditation may take one out of the world, but it also puts one totally into it. The experience of the poem gives both distance and involvement: one is closer and farther at the same time"(1-2). It becomes what it is, a still path for focus and self-realization; most Zen poems are poems of meditation whether in Nature's tranquility or in the midst of life's struggles. Yet Snyder points out the difference between Zen sitting and the writing of a poem: "Meditation looks inward, poetry holds forth. One is private, the other is out in the world. One enters the moment, the other shares it. . . .they are both as common as grass; the one goes back to essential moments of stillness and deep inwardness, and the other to the fundamental impulse of expression and presentation"(2). Snyder also places significance on the value of playfulness in the poetry, ". . . play is essential to everything we do—working on cars, cooking, raising children, running corporations—and poetry is nothing special. . . . The poet in us can be seen at both the beginning and the end of a life"(5). This trust in the wild and original self is part of the "crazy cloud" tradition of play in Zen poetry and practice seen in such models as Han-Shan, Dogen, Ikkyu, Hakuin, Ryokan, Senzaki, and it is clearly in evidence in many of the writers assembled here who celebrate a healthy irrationality in the face of life's struggles, as it once did in the work of e.e. cummings. The poem becomes a way of de-conditioning a dualistic vision by restoring wholeness.

The Zen Aesthetic in Art and Poetry

We know that a certain Zen aesthetic has evolved in the arts of landscape painting, flower arrangement, calligraphy, gardening, flute music, the *feng shui* of layout and design....and in America in "the art of ..." archery, golf, even motor cycle maintenance. What then is the Zen aesthetic developed in the work of these poets? Though American Zen poetry is basically "impure" in its practice, key characteristics and qualities make up its Zen aesthetic. As John Daido Loori points out in his *The Zen of Creativity*, "The creative process, like a spiritual journey, is intuitive, non-linear, and experiential. It points us toward our essential nature, which is a reflection of the boundless creativity of the universe" (1).**

An essential ingredient of Zen art is the "chi" energy or spirit in the work drawn from realizing life's original nature. Another is the trust inherent in the work, the bond of self, subject, reader, and the world. Developed through Zen meditation and breathing practice, it becomes a stance toward reality, assuring the artist that all is already there. "Trust that we have enough, that we *are* enough" (Loori 161) is a fundamental and understood theme. Creating without rules, out of emptiness, the works are spontaneous and intuitive, finding form in the *wu wei* or 'no mind' of Zen. The work evolves without expectation or directed intent, and so achieves a certain "thusness" or "suchness" of experience, without explanation. To explain or interpret causes the reader (viewer) to stare at the finger rather than the moon to which it points. This is one reason for the close and concrete writing of haiku and tanka. Loori asserts truly, "The essence of our lives, the heart of the matter is essentially ineffable"(241). The ego goes out of the work in favor of the Oneness, the small self dissolves into the large Self of all life. This follows the maxim that "If you would paint the plum tree, you must be the plum tree." Poet, word, reality are one, and the resulting work, minus ego, is simple and direct with a barebones simplicity, sparse and non-dual. *Transparent* gets it; so that the reader sees, hears, smells the water flowing as water flowing, but also looks through the water to the rounded stones beneath. Because it is natural, it lacks the slickness and false grace of perfection, capturing instead the ordinary, everyday life in its irregularity and nakedness. Leonard Koren describes this Japanese concept of *wabi-sabi* as "a beauty of things imperfect, impermanent, and incomplete. It is beauty of things modest and humble. It is beauty of things unconventional"(*Wabi-Sabi* 7). Further, the reader is invited into the still circle, to create the poem within, where "Form is no other than emptiness; emptiness is no other than form; form is exactly emptiness, emptiness exactly form" ("The Heart Sutra"). The poem holds the organic shape of experience.

Regarding the subjects of these poems, a few observations can be made. We found we were reading poems of Nature rich in telling images, poems of coming to quiet awareness and awakening, poems of sensing one's life as practice true and false. Many present how one's daily life and one's practice interact. There are poems of youth as well as aging and death, and poems of relationships with family and friends, including lovers. Some engage the topical as representative, as Tu Fu did with his poems of warfare and sacrifice. Most include a deep sense of life's impermanence, and the permanence of change. Our invitation to have the writers make personal statements about their life and work and Zen has produced a living document and testimony to the "chi" spirit of Zen. All of the poems achieve a sense of being in the moment where past and future reflect in the pool of presence. As John Gilgun points out here, "…if Buddhism is anything it is ironic," and poetry has always sought the impossible task of expressing the inexpressible, using all means to help us see the obvious and to realize the ineffable. As Ryokan warned at the beginning here, what we have in Zen poetry is—Not the making of poems as art or the talking about poetry, but the poem itself as being, Dogen's "moonlight reflected in the dewdrops/ shaken from a crane's bill."

On Zen in Translation

America's Zen translators begin with Ezra Pound's working with the notes of friend Ernest Fenollosa, to produce the stunning and lyric volume *Cathay* (1915). Their most often translated poet is Rihaku (Li Po), and so Pound's readers heard the Zen voice in "The River-Merchant's Wife: A Letter": "You dragged your feet when you went out./ By the gate now, the moss is grown, the different mosses,/ Too deep to clear them away!/ The leaves fall early this autumn, in wind./ The paired butterflies are already yellow with August . . . ." Such concrete and lyric lines in which self and nature merge through an absorbed imagery are reflected in Imagist verse, as in Pound's famed "In a Station of the Metro" consisting of: "The apparition of these faces in the crowd;/ Petals on a wet, black bough."

According to translator Willis Barnstone, "The Chinese poets, especially in the Tang (T'ang) and Song (Sung) periods, 'dance in their chains,'—meaning that despite strict forms, the voice comes through as natural, confessional, and candidly conversational—and this overheard quality is especially appropriate to modern American poetry (*The Poem Behind the Poem* 33). These descriptive words "natural, confessional . . . candidly conversational . . . [an] overheard quality" are key to grasping the Zen aesthetic, and revealing of the T'ang Ch'an poets and their model to our modern American poets. As Johnson and Paulinich point out in their preface to *Beneath a Single Moon*, Ezra Pound's fascination with the Chinese and Japanese ideogram, developed into a trust in techniques of "elisions and juxtapositions" as a way of moving a poem internally and yet beyond linear thought (*Beneath* xvii). In fact they suggest Thoreau as an early developer of "projectivist" writing, in which the work derives its original and organic form from the authentic interaction of the poet's outer and inner landscapes. The poet is seen as the open medium for expressing the natural self. Interdependence and interpenetration are assumed in both Zen and the Projectivist verse of such mid-1950's poets as Charles Olsen, Robert Creeley, Robert Duncan, Paul Blackburn, and others.

Because Japanese Zen and Chinese Ch'an derive from three main sources: Buddhism, Confucianism, and Taoism, so Lao Tsu's *Tao te Ching* is a primary element in the development of American Buddhist thought and art. And the first English translations of this ancient document, a poem really, arrived in 1927 from Paul Carus's *Tao te Ching: The Canon of Reason and Virtue* by Lao Tsu (Chicago: Open Court Pub.) and James Legge's *The Sacred Books of China: The Texts of Taoism [Tao te Ching]* (London), followed in 1937 by Ch'u Ta-Kao's *Tao te Ching: A New Translation* (London: Buddhist Lodge). Over 50 English translations have developed since then, most by American Zen poets, including the popular version by D. C. Lau (Penguin 1963) and the illustrated version by Jane English and Gia-fu Feng (Vintage 1972, reissued in 1997). One encounters in Lao Tsu's *Tao te Ching* a non-dualist challenge to discursive thought and a suggestion of a Zen ethic.

Historically the next wave of texts from Asian sources came through Arthur Waley's translations of the classic *Book of Songs* (Boston: Houghton, Mifflin 1936) and his *The Analects of Confucius* (London 1938), followed by his early translations of *Japanese Poetry* (The *UTA*. London 1955). However, many first discovered Buddhist inspired writing through the multi-volume translations of R. H. Blyth's *Haiku* (Tokyo: 1949-1952). The haiku's compact and image based form embodies the Zen aesthetic with its emphasis on being present to and unobtrusively recording the perceived moment of awareness. It has been a key development in the influence of Zen art on American culture and its poets. The other 1940's development came in the form of the *101 Zen Stories*, translated by American Paul Reps and Japanese-American Nyogen Senzaki (McKay 1940), Zen poets and teachers who each represent an original and unconventional spirit.

During post World War II America Reps and Senzaki also did the influential *Zen Bones, Zen Flesh: A Collection of Zen and Pre-Zen Writings* (Rutland, Vermont: Tuttle 1957/1958). The first individual collection of an ancient Ch'an poet appeared in *Poems by Wang Wei* (Tuttle 1958), translated by Chang Yin-nan and Lewis C.Walmsley; to be followed, as we will see, in the decades to come by over thirty collections translating individual Zen poets from the T'ang and Sung Dynasties and their later descendents. By the mid-50s Zen had arrived on the West Coast as the San Francisco Poetry Renaissance welcomed the Beat Movement. On October 13, 1955, Pacifica poets Philip Whalen and Gary Snyder joined with San Francisco's Michael McClure and Philip Lamantia in greeting New York's Allen Ginsberg in the celebrated Six Gallery Reading hosted by West Coast literary guru Kenneth Rexroth, with Jack Kerouac howling from the audience. Their healthy interaction with Buddhism led to Gary Snyder's translations of Han-Shan's Cold Mountain poems (*Rip Rap & Cold Mountain Poems*; S.F.: Four Seasons 1965), and to Kerouac's popular novel of those times, *The Dharma Bums* (Viking 1958) which 'translated' Eastern thought however loosely into a Western landscape and action, giving us Beat Zen.

In the 1960s A. C. Graham produced the ever popular *Poems of the Late T'ang* (Penguin 1965), a book used in classrooms then and today. Large publishers began taking an interest in Zen Buddhism, seen most effectively in Nancy Wilson Ross's seminal collection, *The World of Zen: An East-West Anthology* published by Knopf / Vintage in 1960. This remarkable book which did so much to propagate a Zen outlook and art was guided by D. T. Suzuki, America's earliest interpreter of Zen Buddhism. Nancy Wilson Ross, a novelist and cultural critic from Washington state would become instrumental in bringing Shunryu Suzuki to America and in developing the San Francisco Zen Center. Her *The World of Zen*, which she compiled, edited, and introduced, contains this dedication: "Still it remains my belief that an East-West exploration of Zen's unique philosophy is capable of shedding some light on the enduring dilemma of human existence, and deepening an awareness of mankind's spiritual brotherhood" (ix). It provided the first thoughtful and rich assemblage of Zen writings in English including D. T. Suzuki on Zen and art, Alan Watts on the haiku, and others on the arts of the Zen tea ceremony, gardening, painting, the Noh drama, excerpts from the *Tao te Ching*, Arthur Waley and Paul Reps' works and translations, a section on "Zen in Psychology and Everyday Life" and another on "Universal Zen." It concludes with Watts on "Beat Zen, Square Zen and Zen," poet Gary Snyder's account of his "Spring Sesshin at Shokoku-ji" in Kyoto, and philosopher William Barrett's summation and forecast for "Zen in the West." Forty years later, it remains an essential gate to understanding American Zen.

Another important development was the first of Lucien Stryk's translations in *Zen: Poems, Prayers, Sermons, Anecdotes, Interviews* selected and translated by Lucien Stryk and Takashi Ikemoto (Garden City:

Anchor, 1965) followed by his work with a Japanese contemporary in *After Images: Zen Poems of Shinkichi Takahashi* (Chicago: Swallow Press 1970). Stryk would go on to write his own fine American Zen poetry and to give us such important translations as *Zen Poems of China and Japan: The Crane's Bill.* (Garden City Anchor, 1973, Grove Press 1987) and *The Penguin Book of Zen Poetry* (Penguin 1978).

The 1970s was a strong year for translations, opening with Kenneth Rexroth's *One Hundred Poems from the Chinese* (New Directions 1970) followed quickly by his *One Hundred Poems from the Japanese* (New Directions 1971). Rexroth himself was such a powerful influence on the whole West Coast scene, both during the Berkeley Renaissance of the 1940s and the San Francisco Renaissance of the 1950s and 60s. He represented for many a broad humanism that embraced Buddhism and Christianity, a Nature poet who remained politically engaged, a model which we see in such poets as Diane di Prima, Anne Waldman, David Budbill, and of course Sam Hamill, one of his friends and students. Hardly a poet in this present collection has failed to read his early translations, particularly his work with his cultural counterpart, Tu Fu. The 1970s also brought us *Hiding the Universe: Poems of Wang Wei* (NY: A Mushinsha Book / Grossman 1972) and *Wang Wei: Poems* by G. W. Robinson (Penguin 1973).

This rich East-West cultural milieu describes the world for many of the American Zen poets assembled here, some of whom have done their own translation work. Translation has provided a bridge for Zen to cross for East to West and back again. We thank these poet-translators and list them along with the poets they have translated and their most recent collections: Sam Hamill: (Po Chu-I, Tu Fu, various Chinese and Japanese poets); *Crossing the Yellow River: Three Hundred Poems from the Chinese* (BOA 2000) / Red Pine: (Cold Mountain [Han-Shan], various Chinese and Japanese poet); *Songs of the Masters: China's Classic Anthology of T'ang and Sung Dynasty Verse.* (Copper Canyon 2003) / David Hinton: (Po Chu-I, Tao Ch'ien, Lao Tzu, Chang Tzu, various Chinese poets; *Mountain Home: The Wilderness Poets of Ancient China.* (Counterpoint 2002) / C. H. Kwock and Vincent McHugh: (various) *Old Friend From Far Away: 150 Chinese Poems from the Great Dynasties.* (San Francisco: North Point, 1980) / Stephen Berg: (Ikkyu) *Crows with No Mouths: Ikkyu, Fifteenth Century Zen Master* (Copper Canyon Press 2001) / Hiroaki Sato: (Mijazawa Kenji, Ema Saiko) / Burton Watson: (Han-Shan, Su Tung-P'o) / Dennis Maloney: (Ryokan, various Chinese Zen poets) / Mike O'Connor: Chia Tao and various mountain monks); *Where the World Does Not Follow* with photos by Steven R. Johnson (Wisdom Publications 2002) / Thomas Cleary: (various ancient texts, including Dogen Zenji) / W. S. Merwin:

(various Asian translations); *East Window: The Asian Translations* (Copper Canyon Press 1999) / Kazuaki Tanahashi: (Hakuin, Dogen Zengi) / John Stevens: (Ryokan) / Stephen Mitchell: (Lao Tzu, others) / Larry Smith, with Mei Hui Huang: (Ryokan, various Chinese Zen poets); *Chinese Zen Poems: What Hold Has This Mountain?* (Bottom Dog Press 1998).

- - - - - - - - - - - - - - - - - - - -Notes: -

*Rick Fields' highly readable history, somewhat dated now, can be supplanted by newer books, *The New Buddhism* by James W. Coleman (Oxford Univ. 2002), *Buddhism in America* by Richard Hughes Seager (Columbia Univ. 2000), *Luminous Passage* by Charles S. Prebish (Univ. of California 1999) and the collection *The Faces of Buddhism in America* by Charles S. Prebish (Univ. of California 1998). Recent books by and about the chief Japanese-American Buddhist teachers Shunryu Suzuki and Taizan Maezumi:: *Crooked Cucumber: The Life and Teachings of Shunryu Suzuki* by David Chadwick (Broadway Books 1999), *Branching Streams Flow in the Darkness* Shunryu Suzuki et al (Univ. of California 1999); *Appreciate Your Life: The Essence of Zen Practice* by Maezumi et.al (Shambhala 2001)

**Other Sources on the Zen Aesthetic in Art and Poetry:

Robert Aitken. *A Zen Wave: Basho's Haiku & Zen*. NY: Weatherhill, 1978.

Jane Hirshfield, *Nine Gates: Entering the Mind of Poetry*. NY: HarperCollins, 1997.

Leonard Koren. *Wabi-Sabi: For Artists, Designers, Poets & Philosophers*. Berkeley: Stone Bridge Press, 1994.

John Daido Loori. *The Zen of Creavity: Cultivating Your Artistic Life*. NY: Ballantine 2004.

Sam Hamill. *The Poet's Work: The Other Side of Poetry*. Seattle, WA: Broken Moon Press, 1990; rev. Pittsburgh, PA: Carnegie Mellon University Press, 1998.

Gary Snyder. *Earth House Hold: Technical Notes and Queries to Fellow Dharma Revolutionaries*. NY: New Directions, 1969.

——. *The Practice of the Wild: Essays*. S.F.: North Point Press, 1990.

Frank Stewart, ed. *The Poem Behind the Poem: Translating Asian Poetry*. Port Townsend: Copper Canyon Press, 2004.

Lucien Stryk. "Preface: Zen Poetry" in *Zen Poems of China and Japan: The Crane's Bill*. NY: Grove, 1973.

——. "Introduction" to *Zen Poetry: Let the Spring Breeze Enter*. NY: Grove, 1995.

Anne Waldman. *Vow to Poetry*. Minneapolis, Minnesota: Coffee House Poetry, 2001.

Introduction—Part Two by Ray McNiece

Begin by accepting the impossibility, the absurdity, of defining Zen, let alone American Zen poetics, and understand that paradox as part of the mix. All roads lead to Rome? Well, all dharma become Buddha. Constantly. Everything is mind–mind made of thought, thought of words, and words of breath empty, this world blown away. Start categorizing, putting Zen in a box, and the emptiness of *box* becomes apparent. Box presupposes an inside and outside when there is always only essence. Awakening speaks light, yet even the sun is illusion. *The way that can be spoken is not the true way*, and, equally valid, Po Chu-I rejoins, *How comes it then that Lao Tzu wrote a book of some 60,000 characters?* One does not cancel out the other. Or, to put it in an American idiom, *Do I contradict myself? I contain multitudes.* Zen is not an entity. Nor is a poem. A poem is a medium where poet, poem, and listener merge interdependently as satori. A poem is both the particles of words and the wave of vibration opening wormhole into timelessness.

In keeping with right contemplation and right speech, the Zen poet practices mindfulness by way of words as meditation. Zen and the contemporary American poetry in this anthology share basic tendencies of directness, spontaneity, simplicity, and naturalness. In this they follow tenets of modernist poetics: ordinary "spoken" language, ideas in things (without attachment), line based not on metrics but on breath or more specifically "mind breaths," an openness of form and subject, and form growing organically from content. It all comes down to breath, the acceptance of transience, inevitability of inspiration and cessation that are the hub of emptiness and form, nirvana and samsara simultaneous. Zen poems speak on the verge of deep silence.

The Transcendentalists stand as spiritual antecedents of this ever evolving, hybrid-American strain of Zen. Their efforts to continue the Revolution into aesthetics by overthrowing English hierarchical poetics opened them to adopt and adapt Eastern spiritual traditions that readily took root in the fertile nature of the new nation. Separation of church and state and freedom of religion made this process easier. Emerson's close study of the Gita, embodied in his poem "Brahma," hastened his departure from the Unitarian Church–which allowed him to found a church without walls near the banks of Walden Pond. Thoreau, perhaps the first American Zen monk, with his mantra of *simplicity, simplicity, simplicity,* saw the mass of men leading *lives of quiet desperation* and went to the woods to confront life to its core and truly awaken. His *We must learn to reawaken and keep ourselves awake, not by mechanical aids, but by an infinite expecta-*

tion of the dawn echoes Milarepa's *Everyday we wake into a new life.* Whitman, the spontaneous celebrator of the ordinary with his valved voice and wide-open speech, still provides the best model for reporting the actual: *Do I have some intricate purpose? / Well I have...for the April rain has / and the mica on the side of the rock.* He expresses the timelessness of objects: *All truth wait in all things / they neither hasten their own delivery nor resist it.* You can't push a river. Consider his notion of form and emptiness: *To be in any form what is that? / If nothing lay more developed the quahog and its callous shell were enough. . . .* Like Basho (albeit more effusively) Whitman sees into the heart of and becomes the object he gazes upon: *The sharphoofed moose of the north, / the cat on the housesill, the chickadee / I see in them and myself the same law.* Uncle Walt sees truly, speaks directly, and accepts it all. His vibrant teaching continues to influence the poets herein.

As the dharma migrated through contemporary poetics it passed through Pounds' Imagist efforts to the Beats, guided along by Rexroth and the other scholars and translators. Kerouac's *Some of the Dharma*, originally composed as instructional letters to Ginsburg, provided the impetus for founding Naropa and its disembodied school of poetics and so the blending of Vajrayana traditions with Dogen's methods carried here by D.T. Suzuki. And yet, there being no history, no America, no Beats, dharma is always here and now. Many of the poets in this anthology trace their literary lineage through these strands, a *sangha* that continues to sustain Buddha nature through its varied permutations.

The Thoreauvian way and path of Han-Shan exemplified by Gary Snyder merge with the work of Budbill, Rain Crowe, Hamill, Lojowksy, Schelling, and Gibson. These poets find their habitation far from the madding crowd, are critical of it, and yet are socially engaged. From his Vermont retreat, Budbill wears the crazy wisdom mask of the hermit: *Wealth and power mean nothing here / this is truly an irrelevant and useless life.* Rain Crowe's simple adherence to the task at hand reminds of what Snyder calls the 'real work': *Tired from labor and a body / too old for work / lay another fieldstone on the outward wall.* Hamill's reflections from his hermitage are poignant: *This world is frost on an old man's breath, / memory rushing into memory.* In her Zen statement Gibson sees a knoll house in the woods not so much as a sanctuary, but as a process of engagement and uses John Daido Loori's definition of "refuge": *It means to act without hesitation, without thought of oneself...deep calls to deep.* Like sitting meditation itself, a specific, isolated place helps us practice the continuous present of the dharma wherever we find ourselves.

The Beat tradition and its sometime left-hand path are well repre-
sented here by di Prima, Gilgun, Kuhar, Skrym and Waldman. Di Prima's
lines on darshan, the blessing transfer of energy, are a microcosm of the
gift that all the poems in this collection embody: *It is darshan, blessing/
transmission of some basic joy / some way of seeing/ LIKE A TAN-
GIBLE GIFT IN THE HAND/ in the heart/ It stays with me.* Several
poems express the practice of *ahimsa* (to do no harm) as in Gallagher's
"Choices" when compassion prevents her from cutting down a tree, which
contains a nest to get a better view of a mountain: *I don't cut the other
either./ Suddenly in every tree/ an unseen nest/ where a mountain would
be.* Gibson celebrates plentitude in the Whitmanesque verses of "One Body":
*I rise up from the mown and edible/ debris of the world/ wrapped in a
bright / net of pollen and stars.* Many poems convey the simple accep-
tance of life and death in its very ordinariness, echoing the spirit of Whitman's
lines: *Has anyone supposed it lucky to be born?/ I hasten to inform him
or her it is just as lucky to die, and I know it/ I pass death with the
dying, and birth with the new washed babe...and am not contained
between my hat and boots.* Hamill echoes this in "The Orchid Flower":
*deepest mystery/ in washing evening dishes/ or teasing my wife, who
grows, yes, more beautiful/ because one of us must die.* This ultimate
realization in the face of decay is voiced in Heyen's haiku: *passing through
passing / clouds–cherry pits & squirrel shit/ in my birdbath.*

Though the first American *sanghas* gathered in urban centers on
the east and west coasts, Buddhist communities also emerged in the Mid-
west as in Kuhar's poem "Suburban Buddha, Coffeehouse Christ" where
*on the streets of quiet houses Buddha sits / Buddha mows lawns, Bud-
dha rakes leaves.* That sense of finding glory in the mundane is expressed
by Montag in his *Ben Zen* poems: *O to be a junkman, Ben says / to have
everything no one wants.* Ragain uses Dogen's quote *If you cannot find
truth right where you are, where do you expect to find it,* as a pivot for
his own explorations ending *in yesterday's half frozen cup / of muddy
coffee you left on the porch rail. / Drink it down. Shoulder the morn-
ing. / A clear, blind river runs beneath your feet.* Some of these poets,
Davis, Koeppel, Twichell, Budbill—practice an openness which allows them
to integrate their Judeo-Christian upbringing with Zen. Twichell's lines in
"The Quality of Striving" echo this: *I write by the light of the secret /
Protestant pride of asceticism / the most seductive Buddha of all.*

And always these poems show the inexpressible stillness at their
hearts as in Ronci's line from "Old Monks Drinking": *Every moment in-
cluding this one,a koan. We didn't speak.* Smith's poem "The Calligra-
phy of Birds" rests with its realization of transience in a gust of wind blow-

ing leaves: *Twin comfort of something larger and not leaving a trace.* Waldman's lines in her elegy for Whalen could be all our epitaphs: *mind at least a bit of it, went into ink/ ink came from mineral rock/ went into branch.* So too goes our scripts, natural wonders of eye, paper, blood, sinew, pen, nerve, keystroke.

So this diverse American *sangha* continues to sit and chant amid the frenetic activity of America, a seemingly antithetical environment what with its business of busyness, its lust for fame and fortune, its hurry to make a living driven by the ethos of every man for himself. The Buddhist definition of anger is competition—the very basis of this system. In general, most of America looks on poetry as it does Zen—as a useless, unnecessary waste of time; meanwhile it finds meaning in the superficial flash of televised *samsara,* looking for the new and improved, the bigger and better. And still we sit, write and recite, wide open to a sky full of fiery flowerets comprising the jewel in the lotus. The stars shine from webs spun by Whitman's noiseless, patient spider. We spin forth these filaments, these breaths of light, gossamer strands disappearing.

[July 2004]

Nin Andrews

Biographical Sketch

Photo by Jim Andrews

"I grew up on a farm in Virginia, the daughter of a dairy farmer and an architect. My father, the architect, always dreamt of becoming an artist and envied writers and painters. My mother wanted to be a yogini and liked to stand on her head in the middle of the room. Sometimes I would stand on my head to talk with her. Otherwise I might not have the chance—my mother was rarely still. My father, by contrast, seemed immobile.

"One of my earliest memories is watching my father paint. He would sit on the porch and water color, one painting after another. And each one, he would toss off to the side where it would dry and curl up like a dead leaf. What amazed me was his love for the process, his intensity of focus, that time out of time—when he was, basically, *just painting*. And how he was never satisfied with the results.

"Sometimes, when I think of him then, I realize he was showing me something—that hunger artists have, an urgency, to enter the world more fully, to see more clearly. And yet how judgmental he was (and most are), how hard on himself. I love the saying in Zen that sitting IS nirvana, not that one sits in order to attain nirvana. In some ways, I guess children inherit their parents' dreams. I've become a poet, a yogini and a Buddhist."

Nin Andrews has written several books of poetry including *The Book of Orgasms* (Cleveland State University) and *Why They Grow Wings* (Silverfish). Most recently she edited a book of translations of the French mystic and poet, Henri Michaux, *Someone Wants to Steal My Name* (Cleveland State University Press). Her newest book, *Sleeping with Houdini*, will be out from Tupelo Press in 2005.

Zen Statement

I received my first meditation instruction when I was twelve years old. A free class was offered at the local university. The Vietnam War was in full swing and many of the participants were recent draft picks. I remember the instructor saying that whatever you do, wherever you go, your mind is your own. Peace, freedom, love. . .all these are merely states of mind, readily available to anyone who meditates.

As a Buddhist practitioner, I take great pleasure in sitting still and watching the mind dance, and watching the mind watch itself dance, and then tracing its absurd logic into my poems. After all, who is watching the mind but the mind? Is the mind just a set of mirrors then, reflecting back and forth to infinity? Is there such a thing as a state of being, like a mirror, with no reflection? If so, who looks into it? Does it make any sense even to ask these questions which have no answer? How can I *not* ask? Not wonder?

As Kafka put it, we're like birds in search of a cage. Or like problems in search of a solution. But Zen offers no solutions. Instead its beauty relies on an engagement with the mystery. And that, for me, is magic. I think of meditation and poetry as a way of feeling the wind under my wings, even if I have no clue how to fly. I think all of us yearn to lift off or levitate, if just a little bit. We long for some kind of transcendence. I think that is the gift a poem offers. It's like a hint, a mini-satori or insight, however mundane. For me, even the smallest suggestion or smile can be enlightenment enough.

Nirvana

After you left me, I was so lonely and sad, I became but an apparition, a ghost of who I had been. I took up wearing a veil, tying my long black hair in a knot, and studying Zen with a robed man who only drinks tea when he drinks tea. I dreamt of you as an unrobed man who only makes love when he makes love. When one is drinking tea, the monk informed me, there is no monk and no tea. There is only the drinking of tea. Often when I was sipping my tea, I would close my eyes and feel your fingers combing my hair from its clasp, circling my shoulders and breasts. You could lift me to your lips like a china cup and sip me so slowly, our one night lasted 49 days and 49 nights. In the end, there was no monk, no tea, no woman. I barely remembered your name. In this way I attained nirvana.

Crossing

Suppose the dead can't help looking back, pressing their wings against the glass like giant moths as if they don't get it, that the flesh is a cell, the light a 50 watt bulb. Maybe this dim life of regret is heaven after all. Like seeing you again at dusk, or imagining I do, there in the shadows of pines leaning through my windows, your arms waving in a frantic dance. When you kissed me, my back arcing like a bow, I remember thinking the last kiss is always the best. I read that in a book about Tibetan monks who were paid to practice dying and coming back with news. After a while death became as familiar as a shirt slipped on or off. A kind of love affair, the monks discovered, an unspeakable intimacy. Some monks discovered a death that is just the right size: an ocean designed for the palms of their hands, each thimble-sized wave preparing for flight. Occasionally one got stuck on the other side. Unable to touch the living or leave for good, he would call for help again and again, flailing his arms like the drowning, inhaling the ache in the distance between heaven and earth. I know how he felt, his silent cries, like hot pebbles in the back of his throat.

Zen 101

The first time it occurred to me there are no orgasms in this world,
I was studying Buddhism. My teacher had told me I don't exist.
I am not solid, not even here. I'm just a fantasy in my mind.
I both haven't arrived and am already past, already tomorrow,
already gone. I had no clue what he meant, so he gave me a koan,
something about who was I before I was born. An orgasm, I said
silently, just waiting to happen, but I wondered, if I don't exist,
then how can an orgasm? And what if I was conceived without one?
Suddenly I pictured all the orgasms in the universe, floating
              over`head
like clouds, like angels. Don't ask me why, but I saw them all
as women, nude and in many shapes and colors, so many

like the nudes I examined in this girly magazine once when the man
behind the counter was talking about the Red Sox, not even noticing
me
picking up one that was not in a wrapper, reading an article
promising the orgasm I've never had, and 5 new ways to win HER
back. I wondered what she looked like, which one she was of the
              photos
inside. I flipped through the pages. I kept flipping and flipping.
So many women looking enchanted, lit beneath a spotlight, little
              starlets,
some wearing nothing but wings. I couldn't believe
they were real. I imagined each to be exactly the size of the
              photograph,
maybe 5 by 7 at most, tiny caged women with velvet eyes.
Without their cages, I'm sure they would fly away,

and I really wanted them to. There was something so frightening
about seeing them tiny and trapped. I couldn't get them out of my
              mind,
their wet lips and thighs. I kept thinking maybe the photographer
painted the negatives, adding color and shine. Of course, I decided
there are no women like that, and no orgasms like the promised ones.
They left town long ago. Though every time I make love,

I close my eyes (I can't believe I'm confessing this), and I see one
of those silky blondes, or the brunette with ringlets dangling
      beneath her breasts,
her half-opened cat-eyes looking back or down at me with disdain,
      as if to ask,
Why are you wasting my time? Then she sticks out her tongue.
By the time I open my eyes, she's gone. And I can never decide
which of us is merely a mirage. She? Or I?

Satori

1. Sometimes I would imagine you, standing outside in the dark, peering in the lit windows. I could feel your eyes on my skin, or something soft moving down my arms like pinpricks of rain.

2. Often I felt so lost, I didn't know where to turn. I had no faith in psychics, weathermen and shrinks who think they can predict the future. Instead I would hang out in the waiting room of loss, watching my loss, contemplating loss, not yet living my lost life.

4. Sometimes at night I became a moth, moon-bathing on your screens, pressing my soft brown wings against the metal.

5. When I dreamt of you, you were a stranger, but everywhere you touched me left imprints on my skin, like fingerprints in snow, like tongue marks in frozen custard.

6. Once, when a lover pressed his ears to my chest, I heard, not his heartbeat, but the silent cries of the drowning.

7. I remember the last time you told me, *I am into Zen. I am transcending desire.* But whenever I made love, I could hear you, calling and calling my name, drifting and wheeling overhead.

8. One day I know, the barrier between us will lift. The loss will become me, and me, lost. That will be my satori. Nothing more.

A Philosophical Inquiry into the Nature of the Human Cock

after contemplating a Tibetan Buddhist tanka, a depiction,
my teacher said, of nirvana—or of several nude goddesses
engaged in seated sex.

Five goddesses, permanent residents of the land of pure bliss, discuss the human cock. One remarks, "It's the cock which brings us great pleasure. Like a worshiper at the temple."

"Oh, no," the second responds. "It is not the cock that brings pleasure, but the man behind the cock. The one who decides to worship. The cock is but his bible."

"But you are wrong," says the third. "It is the thoughts of the man behind the cock. The thoughts which inspire him to lift up the good book and read from it. And one cock, like one thought, is never quite like another."

"But you are all wrong," the fourth insists. "The man knows nothing of his cock. Or his own prayers. The cock and prayers know more of a man than vice versa. In truth, a man's cock is not his own. A man is but a stranger to his cock."

"Exactly," agrees the fifth goddess. "A man knows not his own cock. So a man can only imagine it. And what he imagines can never be a cock, but is only an idea of a cock. What a poor substitute for reality illusion, is. A cock removed from a pussy is little more than a thought removed from a mind.

Thus, the real cock, is an only can be, that which begins and ends in the pussy. Which takes, I am sorry to say, about as long as it takes to sip a warm cup of tea."

David Budbill

Biographical Sketch

Photo by Jenny Jimenez

David Budbill was born in Cleveland, Ohio, in 1940, to a streetcar driver and a minister's daughter. "In high school I was most definitely not a good student but excelled at playing jazz trumpet and running track. In college I started an underground literary and political magazine for which I got in a whole peck of trouble with the college administration because they considered a short story I wrote to be pornographic. In 1962 I entered graduate school in theology in New York City. In that same year I bought two used books: *The Essentials of Zen Buddhism* by D.T. Suzuki and a tiny paperback called *A Taoist Notebook* by Edward Herbert which began what has become a lifelong interest in Asian religions and poetry." In the 1960s he was active in both the civil rights and anti-war movements. "The events of 1968 were enough to convince me that 'mere anarchy was loose upon the world,' and I left America for a spot in the remote mountains of northern Vermont where, with my wife, I bought some land and built a house, and where we have been ever since."

After twenty years of writing long narrative poems about people in an imaginary place called Judevine, a third world country within the boundaries of the United States, he began publishing poems inspired by forty years of reading ancient Chinese and Japanese poetry. The first book of these poems, *Moment to Moment: Poems of a Mountain Recluse* (Copper Canyon Press, 1999) will be followed by *While We've Still Got Feet* (Copper Canyon Press 2005).

Statement: "How My Writing Fits the American Zen Spirit"

I was born and raised in Ohio in a working-class family and neighborhood. I grew up deep in the Methodist church. It's a mystery to me how over the years I've become associated with Buddhism and particularly Zen Buddhism. People think I'm a Buddhist. I tell them I'm a Taoist-Buddhist-Methodist. I got interested in "eastern" religions and in Chinese poetry in my early twenties. Those interests are still with me more than 40 years later. I read ancient Chinese poetry almost exclusively. Han-Shan, of all the ancient Chinese poets, has had and continues to have the biggest influence on how and what I write. I don't read much contemporary poetry of any kind. I play a *shakuhachi*, a Japanese vertical bamboo flute, every day. I do a little Yoga too and once in awhile I sit on a cushion kind of cross-legged, burn incense in front of my little homemade altar, and breathe evenly and sit quietly, sometimes for a long time. I don't chant sutras or anything else like that. I live in the remote mountains of northern Vermont where I have every year for the past 35 years cut a year's supply of firewood and raised a year's supply of vegetables. My poetry is about my struggles with ambition and about my fear of aging and death, but it is also about my life here in the mountains, the pleasures and delights of daily life, and the melancholy passing of time.

Tomorrow

Tomorrow
we are
bones and ash,
the roots of weeds
poking through
our skulls.

Today,
simple clothes,
empty mind,
full stomach,
alive, aware,
right here,
right now.

Drunk on music,
who needs wine?

Come on,
Sweetheart,
let's go dancing
while we've
still got feet.

Thirty-Five Miles to a Traffic Light

From here it's five miles to the black top,
thirty-five in any direction of the compass
to a traffic light. People say it's way out there.

I say, yes sirree. Far out, man, say I. Far out
is what it is. Just snow and cold and isolation
and nobody to see for days and days. People get

scared by so much emptiness. So much silence
is frightening. Better not come here if you
don't want to fall in upon yourself. Better yet,

better not come here at all.

Irrelevant and Useless

This place is so remote people call it Nowhere.
Hardly anyone ever comes by—except the clouds.

They visit almost every day. My only neighbors
are the birds, and they don't care what I do.

I play my flutes, read books of poems, work
in my garden, and watch the days go by.

Wealth and power mean nothing here.
This is truly an irrelevant and useless life.

Like Smoke from Our Campfire

All those plans for fame and fortune, honor and glory,
        where are they now?

Drifted away like smoke from our campfire, dissipated
        into the thin, night air,

the fire deserted and gone down to a few ashy coals,
        almost out.

And all of those who sat around the fire: gone away too
        into oblivion.

This Shining Moment in the Now

When I work outdoors all day, every day, as I do now, in the fall,
getting ready for winter, tearing up the garden, digging potatoes,
gathering the squash, cutting firewood, making kindling, repairing
bridges over the brook, clearing trails in the woods, doing the last of
the fall mowing, pruning apple trees, taking down the screens,
putting up the storm windows, banking the house—all these things,
as preparation for the coming cold . . .

when I am every day all day all body and no mind, when I am
physically, wholly and completely, in this world with the birds,
the deer, the sky, the wind, the trees . . .

when day after day I think of nothing but what the next chore is,
when I go from clearing woods roads, to sharpening a chain saw,
to changing the oil in a mower, to stacking wood, when I am
all body and no mind . . .

when I am only here and now and nowhere else—then, and only
then, do I see the crippling power of mind, the curse of thought,
and I pause and wonder why I so seldom find
this shining moment in the now.

Thomas Rain Crowe

Biographical Statement

Photo by Kenn Long

Thomas Rain Crowe, one of the "Baby Beats" of the 1970s San Francisco Renaissance and editor of *Beatitude* magazine, was born in Chicago in 1949 and raised in the Smoky Mountains of Western North Carolina. He is a poet, translator, editor, publisher, recording artist and author of eleven books of original and translated works. His titles include *The Laugharne Poems* (written at the Dylan Thomas Boat House in Laugharne, Wales and published by Gwasg Carreg Gwalch), *Writing The Wind: A Celtic Resurgence (The New Celtic Poetry)* and *Drunk on the Wine of the Beloved: 100 Poems of Hafiz* (Shambhala). He is former Editor-at-Large for the *Asheville Poetry Review* as well as a regular feature writer for the *Smoky Mountain News* and book and music reviewer for several publications including *Jazz News* and the *Bloomsbury Review*. He is founder of the poetry & music band *Thomas Rain Crowe & The Boatrockers*.

His literary archives are collected at the Duke University Special Collections Library in Durham, North Carolina. His memoir *Zoro's Field* documenting four years of self-sufficient living in the wild of the Southern Appalachian mountains from 1979 to 1982 will be published by the University of Georgia Press in the spring of 2005. He currently lives in the Tuckaseegee community of Jackson County, North Carolina.

Statement: The Tao of Zen

> *"If you don't know where you're going,*
> *Any road will take you there."*
> *- George Harrison*

My first introduction to the world of Zen Buddhism came at the age of nineteen following a spiritual experience that probably saved my life. I was looking for answers. In Zen Buddhism there seemed to be plenty of questions, but few answers. The questions kept me going. Six years later, while living in San Francisco during the 1970s, I came across Kenneth Rexroth's *One Hundred Poems from the Chinese*—in which I discovered the T'ang Dynasty poet Tu Fu—which led to my associations with Rexroth, Gary Snyder (from whom I learned of Han-Shan) and Philip Whalen (who introduced me to Ryokan and Lao Tsu).

Since leaving San Francisco in 1979 (where I was writing a lyrical verse of urban angst) for a rural life along the North San Juan Ridge in the California Sierras, and later a *Walden*-like stint in the wilds of the western North Carolina mountains, nature has been at the center of my work. For the past twenty-five years, it is wildness and wilderness that have excited me. And a surging adrenaline drives me to write. To me, the notion of an "American Zen" might imply, simply, a poetry with nature at its center, and that is centered, simple, and yet profound—reflecting a sense of awe, exuberance, humility, The Everything and the Nothing, paradox, and the paramours of darkness and light, preferably all at the same time. In the end, writing poetry is an exercise in humility, I suppose. Seeking no attachment, I am humbled by what comes through me, and sometimes even amazed.

Here on my North Carolina mountain farm along the Tuckaseegee River, I read books on Zen gardens and build "Zen-things" of my own (tori, fountains, bamboo fences, sand gardens....) as my life moves at a slower and more even pace with each passing year. At 55, the "pace" of my poems has changed. "Slow down" I caught myself writing several years ago. Since then, I have written, also, of prayer ("Everything is sacred"), the profound ("How much alike/are the wise man and the drunk"), proclamation ("work is the health of love"), the peaceful ("the lullaby of an ancient kiss"), perception ("the Earth is my body"). Koans that help to clarify my existence and yet leave me with increasingly more questions, fewer answers.

Tuckaseegee, NC/,January, 2004

The Saw-Mill Shack
> *for John Edwards Lane*

I have come to this land,
how many years.
Alone, and for many months,
I have built this saw-mill shack.
Stone stacked and mortared on stone,
logs laid and joyned in joints,
rough oak boards nailed to beams and rafters
with 9" spikes.
Eat lunch each day listening to
rushing stream running over rocks,
through rhododendron, off Doubletop Mountain.
Sound of grouse wings drumming in the woods—
With roof on, windows in,
and woodstove sitting in the hearth,
I stand outside gazing at what
these hands have done.
(An old chimney, still standing and covered in vines,
now a place to live.)
Tired from labor and a body
too old for work.
Lay another flat, smooth stone into the outyard wall.

Occam's Razor
> *for Wendell Berry*

Work is the health of love.
The best path.
Something as simple as wood.
As wild
as a tree. Or
the perfect essence of space—
These ways.
Like the magic of hands:

gone, without trace...

In a small world,
I live with the things I grow.
Careful of what comes.
Letting nothing go.

After Reading Han-Shan
for Gary Snyder

How much alike are the wise man
and the drunk!
The wise man sees the light in the cloud,
the one who drinks: the cloud in the light.
Each seeing the same thing.

How I love the way Han-Shan laughs when he speaks!
And in laughing, the way he cries—
His dreams are like mine: full
of maidens in cloaks of crimson silk.

Wondering today the direction in
which my life will go, the *I Ching* says:
"Where disorder develops, words are the first steps."
No word this time of crossing the great water.
But a message of keeping still.

So tonight I have made myself a cup of tea
and sit with my friends: all the words I know.
Having taken the first step toward tomorrow,
I make a bold stroke with my pen
that in this dim light looks like one
of those court maidens Han-Shan and I know so well.
I sit for a moment in the trance of another world.
Far away from here. But like this small shack in the woods,
still home.

Tools

Silver and slick as velvet
the edge of the old hoe glistens,
      how I've filed away this day—

A Pond in the Woods

There are answers in the ponds at night.
Like the silence of fish.
How many wheels are turning in these woods?
Little lives
unseen in the dark
as I walk alone by the lanternlight presence of moon.
For those who don't die,
their lives are like the time that is locked up in rocks.
Stones thrown sleeping into
the bottom of the pond
where bream bed and are born
to the water in flight.
This night
like remembered moonlight
reflected in the eyes of owls.

Winter Moon Haiku

When the moon
      is in the morning wine:
           delicious!

Kathe Davis

Biographical Sketch

Photo by Candace Davis

"I was born in 1943, a war baby, in Los Angeles—Hollywood, really: Wilshire Blvd. Hospital. I moved with my mother and young Army-Air Force father all over the South, but wherever we were, I knew I wasn't from around there. I started first grade in the Texas Panhandle, took my First Holy Communion in Iowa. When I was eight we settled finally in Algonquin, Illinois, where we swam in the Fox River and roamed freely those woods. I grew up there, and went to the nearby state college. After a go at the Iowa Writer's Workshop and a desk job in Chicago, I went back to Southern California. I wasn't from around there either.

"I got married, got an M.A. in Boston, a Ph.D. in Providence, where my son was born, taught a year in Maine, wrote a year in South Carolina, and landed in Kent, Ohio, in 1976. I spent two different semesters on Cape Cod, and thought *that* was a place I could call home. I loosed my mother's ashes into a storm there one All Soul's Day. But I've had to realize that my people are here; they are Midwestern and so, it seems, am I.

"I wrote my dissertation on John Berryman's *Dream Songs* and continue to ponder the nature of addiction, freedom, gender—not to mention spirituality and, well, home. A word person has to wonder about what language means to all those issues—and what they mean to language. In the Kent State English Department I gratefully teach Women's Literature and poetry of many varieties. Increasingly I find writing poetry more satisfying than commenting on it. Writing, and just reading, for no further purpose than just to savor the words. Maybe finally that's home."

Kathe Davis' poems have appeared in *Phoebe*, *Hurricane Alice*, *Pudding Magazine,* in the Pudding House collection *Fresh Water: Poems of the Rivers, Lakes, and Streams*, and in the commemorative anthology *A Gathering of Poets* (Kent State University Press, 1991).

Zen Statement

Since Zen transcends nationality (among other things), it's funny to think about American Zen. Zen transcends even Zen: Rumi, Patanjali, the Gita, Muhammed, Jesus, the Dalai Lama, Lao Tsu, all offer the small dark light: surrender. They all know we vibrate to the frequency of the static in the uni-verse, in our ears the spiral of the galaxies—this thing bigger than words, that, being human, we keep trying to say. So big—but small, since no thinking is more grounded than Zen in the everyday: chop wood, carry water. Our everyday is inescapably American. Chop hamburger, carry flag. (Though it might have to be the world flag.) Fix your motorcycle. So here I am, hybrid as Zen itself, a Midwestern (German, Scottish, Welsh) collapsed Catholic woman visiting Farther-north America, searching out Gampo Abbey in Nova Scotia in hopes of finding Abess Pema Chodron, American mom and housewife turned Tibetan Buddhist nun. What I found was the sea. It belongs to the country—out to 200 miles, where the water laughs at the boundary. What boundary? Who can say what water's in the wave? The sea reminded me I'd already gotten the requisite knock on the head. When it happened, a foreign sea let me sit still and see what the universe looked like without a bottom. My self smashed, and not yet knowing that a gift, I had poetry to lean on—and the thing that poetry leans on. There was still a universe. I went to the American Atlantic to learn how to make a virtue of emptiness. The sea was my koan: great emptiness, great fullness. I learned dancing by the graveyard. The animals already knew what I was trying to learn. Honor to raccoon, American. Fortunately we are all animals, in the same place we are god. To see the miracle that is the ordinary inspires gratitude. In this starving Land of Plenty, gratitude may be our only salvation. I hope that explains what's Zen in these poems. D. T. Suzuki says, "Human beings talk—this is their will." But "Opinion is the barren flower of the Way." At length, I aspire to silence.

Animal Zen

The raccoons are persistent
and forgetful

every night
they knock
the garbage
can over
though it's empty
empty

Searching for Mooncakes

From Texas by electron
comes advice, Chinese:
"Go get some mooncakes
at oriental market
and celebrate full moon
with your friends, drinking
tea and eating moon cakes, making
wishes to the full moon."
I've learned to cross
when the light says WALK;
I follow these instructions,
or try. Mooncakes, she tells me, "have the yolk
of the pickled duck egg, which is deep yellow,
surrounded by bean paste or lotus paste
with sugar and oil. Some have minced meat,
bits of bacon. They are all very very rich
and very very tasty, thus eaten
in slices and slowly
sampled." I drive
to the Dragon Trading Company.
I've stayed away too long:
tab it's empty, sold.

So a later day I drive State Road
to Oriental Food and Gift,
in the back of the mattress store,
looking for mooncakes.
"Everybody has a hungry heart,"
the radio is singing just as,
where The Cathedral of Tomorrow
thrusts its godly smokestack,
I see the moon. It is
my undaughter's birthday and
the last day of September,
near-record cold.

"I'm not carrying any more,"
the Korean owner says.
"Lose too much money."
So I look at sake sets and buy
sweet-bean-filled rolls
and big flat rice crackers, toasted
the color of the harvest moon.

At the full moon reading,
I share them out to friends,
fiddler and poet; we
crackle cellophane and crunch
the crackers in what is supposed
to be rapt silence of attention
to the music, sad lyrics
and thin strings of baby Dylans.
It's all boys tonight, brave, tender
and bad.

But we are all amateurs.
Mid-Autumn Moon Festival:
not our holiday, not
our culture, but we take
our magic where we can.

"Remember Moon Granma
is the oldest granma around
who's been witnessing
life on earth for ever
as earth has evolved.

"Connect with Her.
Listen to her in your dreams."

We don't know the words
but we can hum the tune.
Missing mooncakes,
we will eat moon.

"The Green Noise of Ohio Hardwoods"

I sit in my woody house
and in the same midnight moment hear
the soft voice of the radio woman
introducing one more genteel
instrumental piece, sure
to come from a safe century ago;
the windchime on my front porch,
yellow plexiglass bird flying perpetually
into the lengths of pipe cut
into harmony by my old neighbor;
and the train:
this railroad town's persistent
romantic distant hooting.

Thus suddenly alerted, I look
at my wood table, wooden chairs,
heavy wood sideboard, light wooden desk.
On a low chair (wood), I lean
against a little wood chest; my foot
rests on the base of the bookcase

that conjoins the central wooden pillars
holding up my house. I am living
inside a tree.
Squirrels come to the windows.

The little ficus from my sister
has stopped dropping leaves.
The looming hemlock never does.
These trees face each other,
outside and in.
I am leafborne, Tschaikovsky borne,
all my treetown grief transmuted
into woody vibrations.

Miracle

Maybe
the burning bush
was just
autumn

It would have been
enough

Diane di Prima

Biographical Sketch

Photo by Sheppard Powell

Diane di Prima has published 42 books of poetry and prose. She began reading Zen classics in the late 1950s, and became a serious practitioner of zazen [sitting] in 1962 when she met Shunryu Suzuki Roshi. She continued to practice Zen for twelve years after Suzuki's death. In 1974, together with Allen Ginsberg and Anne Waldman, she helped to found the poetry program at Naropa Institute, founded by Chogyam Trungpa Rinpoche. In 1983 she became his student and began traditional Tibetan Buddhist practice. She continues to practice and study under the guidance of the Dzogchen teacher Lama Tharchin Rinpoche, who lives nearby on the California coast. Her most recent works include: *Revolutionary Letters* (Revised, Last Gasp Press 2004), *Recollections of My Life as a Woman* (Penguin 2001), *Opening to the Poem* (Penguin 2004), and two chapbooks, *Towers Down* and *The Ones I Used to Laugh With*. She lives in San Francisco where she teaches privately.

Statement on Poetry and Buddhism:

When I look at my life as a writer, it seems that Zen has always been with me in some way. Not to write *about*, but as an attitude of mind that was taken for granted—and was felt to be closely related to the attitude of the artist. Nothing was farther from my mind at that point than actually *sitting*—somehow that was not the point. The POINT at that time had more to do with a mindset—a kind of clear-seeing combined with a very light touch. A faith in *what one came up with*, a sense, as Robert Duncan once said, that "consciousness itself is Shapely"—that, in fact, we know more than we know and simply have to trust it. As you can perhaps imagine, a kind of disattachment goes with this attitude: "you" i.e. your conscious controlling self, don't "make" the work, and so in a curious way you have no stake in it: you have nothing to lose—you don't have to make it into your definition of "good art."

1962 brought me to the West Coast, and to my first meeting with Shunryu Suzuki, who had recently begun teaching in San Francisco. Seeing Suzuki Roshi for the first time was for me the rock-bottom experience of encountering someone whom I knew that I could fully trust. In trying to explain my coming to Zen, I have often said that if what Suzuki Roshi had been doing was apple-picking or welding, that is what I would have taken up. I learned to sit at this time, and when I returned to New York, I brought a zafu and zabuton back with me. Sitting alone in New York was something other than sitting at Sokoji, but I kept at it, sometimes sporadically, and wrote a couple of times a year to Richard Baker, who passed my letters on to Suzuki, and his answers or instructions back to me. And whenever I happened to be in San Francisco on a poetry tour, 5 a.m. would find me hitching to zazen (I didn't drive & buses were few or nonexistent at that hour.)

This went on for about five years, and then finally, seizing an opportune moment when I had some money and my husband (who didn't want to move out of New York) was off in India, I picked up the kids and moved to San Francisco to be close to my teacher. San Francisco was in the heyday of its revolution and my days were filled with distributing free food, writing poems for guerilla theatre, hosting the Diggers and the Living Theatre, and sitting zazen. I sat at Sokoji faithfully every morning at 5:30. For a while four of the fourteen adults in my "communal house" sat, and we could be seen pushing my blue VW bus with its broken starter up Oak Street in the pre-dawn light.

I remember how frightened I was of my first *sesshin* [extended retreat]—Would I be able to do it?—and how intrepidly I went to every sesshin that was offered. As time went on and the Zen Center developed, I had my differences with the community, but none with the practice or with my teacher. He sat with us every morning in the old Japanese temple on Bush Street, while the birds and the city slowly came awake, and after the chants he would stand at the door and bow individually to each and every one of us, scrutinizing us keenly but gently as we left. I felt that nothing escaped him, and that the manner of our bows, the hesitation, self-consciousness or bluff we presented as we set out, told him everything about where we were "at."

There were, too, the private interviews—*dokusans*—at every sesshin, and at other times as we requested. The instruction given at my first interview was to form my deepest question in such a way that it would express the totality of my understanding, as it was at that moment, to my teacher. The bow, the question, asked the same thing of me that the poem did: that I render utter trust to myself, as I was, knowing that I knew more than I knew. This surrender to what Roshi called Big Mind is what I had felt from the beginning to be required of me as a writer; it was with this understanding that I came to the cushion. Yet I must add that in some ways I am very backward: it is only now (thirty years later) that it has come to me that this same approach can also be brought to bear in my daily life.

I learned much more than I know—even now—from Shunryu Suzuki Roshi in the few years that I lived close to him. At the last "lay ordination" ceremony in 1971, I received a name from him which I treasure to this day: Kenkai Banto means, I am told, both "Inkstone Ocean, Ten-thousand Waves," and "Inkstone Mother, Ten-thousand Children" (in that ocean and wave in this particular relation also stand for mother and child). My friend and teacher Katagiri Roshi also laughingly translated it as "Ocean (or Tempest) in an Inkstone, Ten-thousand Poems."

After my teacher's death, I found the differences I had with Zen Center to be more than I knew how to deal with: my anarchism was at odds with their necessary organization. I continued to sit "on my own" however, rather rigorously, relying on teachings I could receive when "on the road." Most particularly, I would seek out Katagiri Roshi in Minneapolis, Chogyam Trungpa Rinpoche at Naropa Institute, and Kobun Chino Roshi wherever I could find him.

DOKUSAN: Visit to Katagiri Roshi
(early 1970s)

Minneapolis.
We talk of here & there
gossip about the folks in San Francisco
laugh a lot.   I try
to tell him (to tell someone)
what my life is like:
the frightened students, the trying
          to sit zazen in motels;
the hunger in America like a sponge
          sucking up
whatever prana & courage
"Pray to the Bodhisattvas" sez
          Katagiri.

I tell him
that sometimes, traveling, I am
too restless to sit still, wiggle &
          itch. "Sit
only ten minutes, five minutes
at a time" he sez—first time
it has occurred to me that this
wd be OK.

As we talk, it becomes clear
there is some continuity
in my life; I even understand
          (or remember)
why I'm on the road.

As we talk
          a transfer of energy
takes place.
It is *darshan*, blessing,
transmission of some basic joy

some way of seeing
LIKE A TANGIBLE GIFT IN THE HAND
     In the heart.
It stays with me.

I Fail as a Dharma Teacher

I don't imagine I'll manage to express *Sunyata*
in a way that all my students will know & love
or present the Four Noble Truths so they look
delicious
& tempting as Easter candy. My skillful means
is more like a two by four banging on the head
of a reluctant diver
I then go in and save—
what pyrotechnics!

Alas this life I can't be kind and persuasive
slip the Twelve-part Chain off hundreds of shackled
housewives
present the Eight-fold Path like the ultimate
roadmap
at all the gas stations in *Samsara*

But, oh, my lamas, I want to
how I want to!
Just to see your old eyes shine in this Kaliyuga
stars going out around us like birthday candles
your Empty Clear Luminous and Unobstructed
Rainbow Bodies
swimming in and through us all like transparent
fish.

Summer Retreat: Pema Osel Ling

Flies, spilled tea,
lost pencils, babies underfoot,
the scramble to bow
to find a seat   then
Lama enters:

The perfect
time   place   teacher
teaching   &   assembly
constellate
               in the light.

[July 7, 1999]

**Poem on the Limits for My Writing Group
Atlantic Center for the Arts
New Smyrna Beach, Florida**

I'll never be able to tell you why it's funny
or sad @ the same time
& how that's OK.
I won't leave my footprints in rock
or help you swim toward your demons.

I don't want to leave you w/a bunch of poems
& w/out the Elixir.
I want to see you burn
& not for love. Be brave
when there's no need for it

honor the hags & children in your pores.
But all I'll be able to do I guess is some renga
maybe a pantoum or death song—
a temporal gesture
that barely scars the ice in your Land of Snows.

Three "Dharma Poems"

1.
his vision or not?
gone is the authority
w/ which he opened his fan.

2.
raindrops melt in the pond
& it's hard to say
just what "lineage" is

3.
my faith—
what is it but the ancient dreams
of wild ones in the mountains?

Stanford M. Forrester

Biographical Sketch

Photo by Emmanuel Paris-Bouvret

Stanford M. Forrester was born in Staten Island, New York, in 1963. In his early teens he practiced Judo and was there introduced to Asian philosophy and Buddhism. His interest in Buddhism became a regular practice upon joining the Peace Corps in Ecuador in 1985. "I lived high up in the Andean Mountains and had plenty of time to develop a practice and work on my own poetry." He completed a master's degree and Ph.D course work in Spanish literature before leaving Boston College. He then worked at Yale University Press for eight years and took some time off to return to the martial arts and earn a second degree black belt in Kempo Karate.

He now lives in Wethersfield, Connecticut, with his wife, Mary and his two daughters, Abigail and Molly. He works at Wesleyan University as an Asian Studies Coordinator and remains active in haiku and in his Buddhist practice. Stanford's Dharma name is Bao Quang, which is both Chinese and Vietnamese for "Treasured Light" and is a member of the Hai An Pagoda which follows in a Chinese/ Vietnamese Pure Land tradition that heavily draws upon Zen. The abbot of the temple is Dharma Master Thich Tri Hoang.

The author is past president of the Haiku Society of America, and the founding editor of *bottle rockets: a collection of short verse*. His work has been published in seven countries and has appeared in 17 anthologies. In 2003 one of his haiku took first seat in the English category of the 57th Annual Basho Anthology Contest in Ueno, Japan. From 2001-2004 Stanford has been one of the judges for the Japan Society's annual haiku contest in New York City.

Zen Statement:

I'm not sure why I have been so drawn to haiku. Perhaps it is because Buddhism and haiku share many of the same key concepts such as impermanence, the interconnectedness of all things, non attachment and being in the moment. In my view, practicing haiku is no different than practicing Buddhism. They both have a certain way of looking at the world. I think the famous Japanese haiku poet, Nagata Koi (1900-1997), whose haiku career spanned over eighty years, would agree, for he writes in *A Dream Like This World* : "I have long wondered, in my own way, whether haiku might not be a philosophy. At least, I think it's good for haiku to retain, in some form or another, some trace of a philosophical shadow. At the same time, I continue to think that haiku is also a religion. If the contemplation of life and death is the basis of literature, then we can call haiku religious in the sense that it is always a means of seeking for a way to live, and to discover and express truth, goodness and beauty." As all things are interconnected, I believe I've learned a lot from Nagata Koi's writings and poetry as well as those by Santoka Taneda who also did not separate his poetry from the path.

One characteristic of Zen, if you can nail down any, is that of humor. I try not to take myself too seriously so I can enjoy as much of the difficult journey as possible, and this attitude tends to be present in much of my work. I remember seeing a while back a Zen scroll with the words "Laugh at this!" What is "this"? My guess, that it is everything. So now I "Live by this!"

One can also see in Buddhism and haiku an interconnectedness in all things. Many times it is present in the space that bridges the first part of the haiku and the second. If one looks closer, one realizes that it is this bridge that connects everything in the universe even if they seem opposite to each other. Are not the Zen master and the haiku poet perfectly comfortable in a world of opposites and juxtapositions? For both of them, being in the moment is key to being aware. When this occurs, we every once in a while get a glimpse of enlightenment that maybe comes as fast as it goes, but it comes. This perhaps describes also the haiku moment.

Haiku

meditation hall . . .
an ant carries away
my concentration

morning light—
all the stone buddhas
robed in gold

only one flower
is needed to answer
your question

daylight…
no one notices
the firefly

temple ruin—
pieces of a buddha
still praying

how quickly
it comes back . . .
dust

dog shit
or me
the fly doesn't care

backyard sun shower—
the windchime song
changes with each cloud

just within my reach   the lightning bug   turns **off**

monk's bowl—
one grain of rice
one ant

autumn wind—
only the stink bug
clinging to me

winter wind—
the length
of the homeless man's beard

melting   into pure water   the snow buddha
moss garden   on the stone buddhas   the sound of rain
mountain wind   prayer flag shadows   on the snow

gray autumn sky—
the blackbirds
turn and turn

a stone
i saved
casting stones

temple bell ringing
one thousand times . . .
winter rain

end of summer . . .
the sunflower disappears
seed by seed

summer afternoon . . .
the first drops of rain
on my bare feet

writing a haiku
in the sand . . .
a wave finishes it

winter afternoon—
a slow shadow fills
the empty bowl

sun on the windowsill…
the dead bee
no longer yellow

plum blossom breeze—
the stone basin
fills with clouds

Tess Gallagher

Photo by Teresa Olson

Biographical Sketch

Tess Gallagher, born during WWII and raised in Pt. Angeles, Washington, the eldest of five children, also spent many summers on her grandparent's thousand acre farm and cattle ranch in the Missouri Ozarks where she learned to ride bareback and explored caves, river bottoms and oak groves.

She is presently completing a poetry manuscript entitled: *Dear Ghosts,* (the comma is part of the title) forthcoming from Graywolf Press. With her Irish companion, the storyteller and painter, Josie Gray, she continues to arrange gallery presentations in America and in Ireland of her poems and his paintings. Gallagher's ongoing fiction project of the past six years is a collaboration with Gray to present written forms of his oral stories from the West of Ireland. Their working title is: *The Courtship Stories.*

Gallagher's most recent books are the essay collection, *Soul Barnacles:Ten More Years With Ray* (University of Michigan Press, 2000), *At the Owl Woman Saloon* (story collection, Simon & Schuster, 1999), *Portable Kisses* (poems, Bloodaxe Editions/Dufour, 1996), *Moon Crossing Bridge*, (poems, Graywolf Press, 1992). Her writing and influence have become increasingly collaborative, dating from her ten year life with Raymond Carver. Her 45 year friendship with the Mexican painter Alfredo Arreguin led to work with him on *ALFREDO ARREGUIN, Patterns of Dreams and Nature,* (University of Washington Press, 2002). She attributes this predilection for collaboration to the wish to "decentralize the ego."

She has published 43 volumes of poetry, fiction, non-fiction, essays and translations, film scripts (*Short Cuts* with Robert Altman and Frank Barhydt, 1993, Capra Press), including four of her late husband's posthumous poetry and prose collections. Her own work is currently being translated into Farsi in Iran and Croatian, and exists in eight languages including Czech, Norwegian and Japanese.

Gallagher recently received an Honorary Doctorate from Hartford University and a Lifetime Achievement Award from the Washington State Poets Association. As the widow of internationally known short story writer Raymond Carver, she continues to be involved daily in all that pertains to his work. She will travel to England and Oregon this year to see productions of his stories as plays.

Statement for Tess Gallagher

Although Tess Gallagher lists here some of her publications, she wishes not to indicate these as "accomplishments," but rather as the accumulations of a life time spent as a writer. She grew up in the logging camps of the Pacific Northwest where her father, a "faller"/ "spar tree rigger" and her mother, a "choker setter," earned the living. Her deep love of and loyalty to forests is perhaps corrective to that time.

Like many raised during the 60s, she became aware of Zen through Alan Watts, followed by over forty years of reading and daily reapproachments to the practice of Zen and most recently, the mindfulness practices of Thich Naht Hahn.

She terms herself a "kitchen buddhist" and even a "failed buddhist." The former points to an altar set up on her kitchen counter. This term also indicates her self-styled and "admittedly undisciplined" approach to bringing Buddhism into her writing and her caretaking for the past 16 years of her mother, in ill health and recently in stages of alzheimers. She also often delights in taking care of her great nephew, Tiernan Barber, for doses of "new mind" and enjoys feeding hummingbirds and squirrels, and Zen gardening. She considers herself a "failed" Buddhist insofar as she feels unapologetic for her "mouse-nibbling-at-the-cheese" way of discovering her changing notions of Zen and Buddhism as it relates to how to live and write.

In 1991 she met the Japanese Buddhist nun and novelist, Jyakucho Setouchi San, in Kyoto and the two struck up an important friendship that has twice been celebrated with publications of their conversations in the oldest women's magazine in Japan. In 1989 she met Peter Matthiessen for the first time and subsequently used elements from his *The Snow Leopard* in her *Moon Crossing Bridge*. Her Zen thinking and Buddhist readings became prominent in her teaching of poetry writing at the Poetry Center at Bucknell University in 1997.

Most recently she spent a week, accompanied by poet Holly Hughes, during Thich Naht Hanh's walking and sitting meditations at the 2004 winter retreat at Deer Park Monastery near San Diego. She appreciates greatly his sense of working not so much against war as FOR peace, although she did appear in *Poets Against the War*, for she believes in an "engaged" form of Buddhism. She lives on Deer Park, east of Pt. Angeles, Washington, and rides her bicycle to Sky House nearby to write. Her friendships with several Irish poets, writers and painters, Ciaran Carson, Mebdh McGuckian, Michael and Edna Longley and Sean McSweeney are some of her most formative, nourishing relationships.

Choices

I go to the mountain side
of the house to cut saplings,
and clear a view to snow
on the mountain. But when I look up,
saw in hand, a nest is clutched in
the uppermost branches.
I don't cut that one.
I don't cut the others either.
Suddenly, in every tree,
an unseen nest
where a mountain
would be.

Not a Sparrow

Just when I think the Buddhists
are wrong and life is not mostly suffering,
I find a dead finch near the feeder.
How sullen, how free of regret, this death
that sinks worlds. I bury her near
the bicycle shed and return to care
of my aged mother, for whom suffering
is such oxygen we do not much
consider it, meaning life at any point
exceeds the price. A little more. A little
more. Each day cheats eternity
by having its all.

That same afternoon, having restored balance,
I discover a junco fallen on its back, beak
to air, rain pelting the prospect. Does
my feeder tempt flight through windows?
And, despite evidence, do they
accomplish it?

Digging a hole for the second bird, I find
the first gone. If I don't think "raccoons"
or "dogs," I can have a quiet, unwitnessed
miracle. Not a feather remains.
In goes the junco. I swipe earth over it,
then set a pot on top. Time
to admit the limitations of death as
admonition.

Still, two dead birds in an afternoon
lets strange sky
into the mind: birds flying through windows,
flying through earth. Suffering must be
like that too: full of loopholes
where the mind watches the hand level dirt
over the emptied grave and,
overpowered by the idea of wings, keeps right on flying.

Sah Sin

I found the hummingbird
clutched in torpor
to the feeder on the day
my one-time student
appeared. I sent him into
the house and tried to
warm it, lifting my blouse
and caching it, (as I'd heard
South American women did)
under a breast.

It didn't stir, but I held it there
like a dead star for awhile
inside my heart-socket
to make sure, remembering the story
of a mother in Guatemala

whose baby had died
far from home. She pretended
it was living, holding it
to her breast the long way
back on the bus, so no one
would take it from her before
she had to give it over.
When the others on the journey
looked across the aisle
they saw only a mother and
her sleeping child, so tenderly
did she hold the swaddled form.

Miles and miles we flew
and I only knew what
that breast was for
all these years when the form
of your not-there arrived. We
were impenetrably together
then, as that mother must have been,
reaching home at last, her child
having been kept alive an extra while
by the tender glances
of strangers.

When I went inside
my student and I found
a small cedar box
with a Nootka salmon
painted onto its glass lid.
I told him about all the dead
hummingbirds I'd heard people
in the Northwest saved
in their freezers because
they found them too beautiful
to bury. We made a small mausoleum
for Sah Sin under the sign

of the salmon, so the spear of her beak
could soar over death awhile longer.
Next we propped the box
on the window ledge
facing out toward the mountains.

Then we went on about
our visit. My student
had become famous in the East
for his poems. Now he was
a little bored with being
a poet. He asked some questions
about what I might be
writing—courteously, as one
inquires about someone
unheard of for awhile.
I made some tea
and served it in the maroon cups
the size of ducks' eggs
so it would take
a long while to drink. Fame.
It was so good to sit
with him again. He seemed
to have miraculously survived
everything to make his way
to my house again.

Heart-Mirror

A little spit on the heart-mirror—
like my father, the gambler,
spitting into his palms
then rubbing them together
before he lets go
the dice. I am rolling
through the stars

just thinking about it.
And my heart, rubbed clean
with maniac luck,
gets what it wanted
for once: this child's moon
and three sentinel lovers.

Mixed

Chewing squash
under stars
a little starlight
gets mixed with
the squash. Does
starlight enhance
the squash or
squash the starlight?

(Deer Park Monestery/ Winter Retreat/ 2004)

Margaret Gibson

Biographical Sketch

Photo by Christina Galesi

Margaret Gibson lives on thirty acres of woods and wetlands just within the southern boundary of the Pawcatuck Borderlands in Connecticut, in a house she calls "Tapovanam." "My closest neighbors are deer, wild turkey, an occasional bobcat, and in spring two pairs of scarlet tanagers." Born in Philadelphia in 1944, she was raised in Richmond, Virginia, educated at Hollins College and the University of Virginia, and came north to Connecticut in 1975. David McKain, whom she married, had built a small house in the woods, and after living three years in New London—where she worked in the Puerto Rican neighborhood, the inspiration for her book *Memories of the Future*—she and her husband and his children Josh and Megan moved out to Preston. "All but one of my books have been written there." Currently she is Visiting Professor at the University of Connecticut.

"After years of reading and sitting in a variety of meditative disciplines, in 1992 I began attending Ocean Zendo on Long Island, where Peter Matthiessen is the Roshi. I received *Ju-Kai* in June, 2000, and continue to take the ferry over to the zendo as often I she can."

Her eight books of poems, all published by Louisiana State University Press, include *Long Walks in the Afternoon*, the Lamont Selection for 1982; *Memories of the Future, The Daybooks of Tina Modotti*, which won the Melville Cane Award in 1986, and *The Vigil*, a Finalist for the National Book Award in Poetry in 1993. Her most recent books are *Earth Elegy* (1997), *Icon and Evidence* (2001), and *Autumn Grasses* (2003).

Statement: Taking Refuge

Watching from my house on a knoll in the woods as snow thickly falls, I see on a branch of the old oak at the edge of the field a red-tailed hawk, motionless but for an occasional swivel of its head. Wind ruffles the neck feathers; the folded wing feathers show patches of white. Flake by flake the hawk is becoming a carrier of snow, a snow hawk. I watch hawk watch the field. I take refuge with the hawk, joined in a wordless partnership that magnifies and clarifies this breath by breath *being with*. My eyes yellow; wind rustles the shawl of feathers my neck now is—and then the great bird lifts and flies off in a broad arc east.

I bow to the empty bough, to the eye that watches, to the essential presence watching with me, whatever it is. *What is it?* Then I go to my desk and write down words that begin to make a poem.

Is this watching, this wording *American?* Is it *Zen? American*—that word today is entangled in trappings of power and greed, a preemptive egotism that is chilling. Zen practice awakens me to the one body that hawk snow oak house and watcher in the house inhabit together. In that undivided quiet, there is no *American*, no *Zen*, no *I*—only indigenous spirit, intimate refuge.

Daido John Loori says that *refuge*—in Japanese *kie-ei*—does not mean protection or safe harbor. It means to act without hesitation, without thought of oneself. In self-forgetting, a transformation takes place. It just comes to you. Deep calls to deep. We have this life. *What is it?*

Strange Altars

*Who sends the mind to wander far? Who first drives life to start on
its journey? Who impels us to utter these words? Who is the Spirit
behind the eye and the ear?*

To steady my heart I say these words, to keep me
     each morning
before the altar in my study, a footstool

     on which I have placed
the head of the Buddha, the gilt rubbed off,
     one lowered eyelid worn gold.

Fixed to a spike, the head of the Buddha's
     fit to a small wood block
for balance, not for permanence—the body of the Buddha

     gone its own way, the head
changed from temple plunder to exotic fragment,
     a bit of inscrutable ruin.

The topknot of flame, the *unisha*, geysers up
     like a gothic spire
from the skullcap of close corkscrew curls.

     Ears pendulous, nostrils
flared, eyebrows the wings of a seabird
     afloat on a thermal. And the mouth,

I love the mouth, how it's puckered in the loose
     serenity of a smile that lingers
when one's been kissed, the lover no longer

there in the room.
And so I sit, *certain of nothing*—some mornings
not even that.

Who sends the mind to wander far—who brings it
home? You think
this asking is easy? A rationed calm? An abeyance,

flowing and cool?
Eat the question, you swallow fire—a ruthless,
unoathed fire that

swallows you completely. Exactly what I want,
the head of the Buddha
rests on the white rebozo I bought in Oaxaca—

rests on a remembered
aroma of sweat and dust and dried herbs in a basket,
ropes of *chile de arbol*

red as the shriek of the small pig hoisted behind
a bright blind
of zinnias and callas, its throat about to be cut.

Summer Birds and Flowers (II)

I don't know just why
but mountains rest on the bend
of a grass blade, blue
A bird in a narrow mask
scalds the air with its scolding

I take refuge in
second-bloom roses, asters
tiny volcanoes

of sun in their ripe centers
It's nearly over, summer

A scroll on a wall
is an open window—one
simply looks and looks
Who dies? Who dies? Who suffers?
Who's born in this absolute

stillness? *No one's home*
But now the tempter steals in
I don't know just why
Perhaps it's always here
softly scolding, the old wish

to be good, be good
Just this spring, drunk with its scent
spellbound by the need
to be more near, I opened
the windows out, transparent

I would drink it in
all day, the heart of the world
And at dusk walked out
to find below the blunt glass
a bird, its eye white as milk

(From Shikibu Terutada, *Summer Birds and Flowers,*
one of a pair of hanging scrolls)

Woman Resting on a Bundle of Kindling

She has squatted down
on her sore haunches to rest
Her chin on her arms
arms folded on the toppled
bundles of kindling, her only

harvest, and that too heavy
Her hands are inside
the sleeves of her kimono
as if held close to a fire
to the very source of fire

and its blossoming
She's allowed her eyes to close
Oh, but do not think
she dreams of horses to lift
her beyond the far mountains

awash with blue mist
A moment's rest, limitless
as wild Kyushu
(the waste land she is given
to glean) will more than suffice

How intimately
how deeply she knows the heart
That it may falter
but does not cease to open
Is dormant, then leafs out green

Whenever I am barren
sated with pleasure or grief
I enter her heart
and know its life is the one
I choose over and over

One Body

I am born in a field
of cornflowers and ripe wheat
     wind in the black gum trees
          late afternoon before the storm
and the men are cutting the field
     working the mower in circles
          coming in and in
toward the center of the field
     where I crouch down
          with the rabbits, with the quail
driven into this space by the clackety mower
     because I want to see
          how the body goes still
how the mind, how the lens of the eye
     magnifies to an emptiness
          so deep, so flared wide
there is everywhere field and the Source
     of field, and only
          a quiver of the nose
or the flick of a top-knot feather, a ripple
     so faint I may have imagined it, says
          yes, says *no*
to the nearing rustle in the last stand of wheat—
     and now it's quiet, too quiet
          a soft trample
a click, the cocking sound, a swish
     as the men steal in to take
          what they want
they are clever, they are hungry
     and because this one body is
          my birthplace
my birthright, my only home place
     my nest and burrow and bower
          I understand
my mother is wheat, my father is wind

and I rise in a tall gust
      of rage and compassion
I rise up from the mown and edible
    debris of the world
      wrapped in a bright
net of pollen and stars, my thighs
     twin towers of lightning
      and my voice
I am a storm of voices, snipe and wolf
     snow goose, dolphin, quail, and lark—
      Stop this. Stop it now
I say to the men, who stalk closer
    keen on the kill, late light
      on the steel of their rifles.
And they are my brothers—they are my brothers
    and I love them, too.
     Look into my eyes,
I tell them. *See for yourself the one shining field.*
   Look into my eyes
     before you shoot.

John Gilgun

Biographical Sketch

I was born and lived until I was twenty-one in a blue-collar Irish-Catholic suburb of Boston called Malden. Could any place be less Zen? On the other hand, perhaps the essential emptiness of life there led me inevitably to Zen. I was desperate as a child for something to believe in and Malden gave me only the void. Zen Malden. Imagine. I was on the road to Zen Emptiness there from birth.

Influenced by Jack Kerouac's *The Dharma Bums*, I took a seminar in Zen Buddhism at the University of Iowa in the spring of 1960. Each student in the class had to have a project. Halfway through the class I told the instructor that my project was to hitchike to San Francisco to see if Kerouac got it right in *On the Road*. The instructor told me that if I made it to San Francisco he'd give me a B. I did make it to San Francisco, but he didn't give me a B. He gave me an Incomplete. I've been trying to make up that Incomplete for the past forty-four years. Could anything be more Zen?

John Gilgun's most recent book is *In the Zone: The Moby Dick Poems of John Gilgun* (Pecan Grove Press, 2002).

Statement: Zen and Poetry and Irony

I can take everyday objects—and Zen is a philosophy which stresses the everyday—and give them structure through Buddhism. It amuses me to create structure through a philosophy which depends on a belief in the absence of structure. I like the idea of creating an object with a word at the same time that I'm saying not only is the object not the word but it doesn't exist except in my consciousness. My poems have shape because of a philosophy that questions the idea of shape. They have meaning because of a philosophy that questions meaning. They are there on the page because of a philosophy which says there is no page there. There is only the word for page. What lies beyond the word is the absence of the word. Buddhist philosophy gives a numinous quality to my poems, "revealing or indicating the presence of divinity." Yet they grow out of a philosophy that questions the idea of anything divine. I love irony and if Buddhism is anything it is ironic. I like humor and I think it is healthy to laugh. If Buddhism is anything it is humorous and Buddhists, who must be the healthiest people on the planet, laugh all the time, like the Zen monk Jitoku sweeping up the laughing leaves that fall from the plum tree with his giggling twin broom.

Buddha Is Lord of Our Town
—For the Edge City Poets

Because he has swept the creeks of consciousness
clean.

Because he has returned the Diamond Estates to the
Diamond Sutra.

Because he has stepped through the mirror of Ego
and brought back MU.

Because he smiles in the silence at the center of
our lives.

Because he loves the rag rug on the railing of the
sagging porch.

Because he sees into the throat of the barking dog
and laughs.

Because the smoke rising from the chimney of the shack
is holy to him.

Because the pick-up truck, the rifle rack and the beer can
are holy to him.

Because the smell of frying bacon
is a communal prayer.

Because consciousness has cracked like ice on the Missouri
and, look, the sun is rising.

Because the air is sharp, cold and crystal clear.
My private pain is gone. And we are here.

Lights Out

Sometimes a child will bring it to consciousness
by coming toward me with a lighted candle in a dish.
"The candle represents safety," I tell her. "Carry it
to the top of Mount Meneguba and place it on a rock
                    as a guide for travelers."

The child answers, "But there are six active volcanos
and frequent earthquakes and seismic seas, waves
and ash rain and flaming clouds and foaming lava flows."
So I lean forward, blow out the candle and ask her,
                    "Where is the light now?"

Zen Frost

You're a flake of frost on the deck.
Your life will be over by noon.

Gone like a sled with red runners.
Gone like red mountains, red dust.

Talk to the frost on the deck:
"Every exit is an entrance somewhere else."

But colder than, colder than....
Oh colder than the bones of Ambrose Bierce.

Zen Sky

Until mind and sweetgum are the same thing,
or the drooping panicle, breathing greenly,
fuses with the clustering orange winged fruit,
                    I am incomplete.

Until flowers of emptiness, casting shadows
on the lawn of non-existence, disappear,
melding with eternity, waking us up,
                    I remain asleep.

Stonechats have stolen the stars, magpies
the moon, serpent eagles the galaxies, leaving
the sky limestone white, cleansed and empty,
                    a massless particle, like me.

Netta Gillespie

Biographical Sketch

"My first poem was published in our local smalltown newspaper when I was 9. Many years later, after raising three children and taking early retirement from my day job and my various volunteer activities, I have finally decided it might be 'OK' to give my prime time to writing. Over the years, I have probably published sixty poems (plus a few stories and essays), some in respected journals, others in mimeographed publications long since defunct. Perhaps it is because I studied writing with Yvor Winters, but I do have a firm belief that poetry, along with beautiful words, rhythms, and sounds, should be meaningful in an ethical and spiritual sense, something that hopefully provides some solace, hope, and perspective to the reader—and conceivably might help even one fellow human get through a rough time. I aspire to this, because it is the role that all the great poems I have read and loved have played in my own life—not always solely, I have to admit, through strength of message, but sometimes also through sheer beauty of expression or because they can make me laugh with delight.

"I don't ever think about Zen when I write. It's just a part of this person who is writing. In my poem about the bus driver, I never thought of the driver as a metaphorical Zen teacher or practitioner. The poem was written about an actual bus and a particular woman driver who brightened the transit time of her passengers, and was once rewarded by a passenger who brought her a rose in the midst of a very cold and snowy Illinois winter. She was an inspiration to all of us en route to dull and repetitive jobs, demonstrating, not preaching, that in any job or work we can work at least small miracles. We who write poetry can hope occasionally to create a small miracle for some reader somewhere. And that's enough. More than enough."

Statement: 'Me—Zen—Poetry'

I was raised a Middle-Western Presbyterian and meandered through long years of seeking before encountering Buddhism, which never asked me to compromise my intelligence and (unlike clergy or college professors) never turned an offended ear to my impertinent questions. It has been ever since like encountering a cold pure spring in a desert. Though I have never found "my" teacher, this has allowed me to learn from a few teachers face-to-face and many others through reading and studying. Now I feel that even if someone burned all my books and closed all the Zen Centers I could get to, there is nothing to lose, nothing to gain.

I believe all forms of Buddhism have the same basic beliefs and goals. I have practiced Zen formally for the past two decades because that was the most accessible path in my circumstances. The essence of American thought and belief is pragmatism, and I agree with William James that, with respect to all religious or philosophical beliefs, "By their fruits ye shall know them" (a phrase borrowed, of course, from Matthew) is the great touchstone. It follows that I think American Zen is a loving and tolerant path that never allows its practitioners to feel that they have the only passport to religious realization, or to be scornful or afraid of different perspectives, let alone inspiring them to hate or violence on behalf of their own views. So if I were to set out to write a Zen poem, I wouldn't make a big point of it being 'Zen.' A poem is a poem.

Seated in a Chinese Painting, He Speaks

This is simple enough: I am seated
On a log under banana trees, writing;
Fish nibble black clouds in the lake
Where my servant washes the ink stone;

And there are always mountains,
More or less misty, perhaps a bridge
To a distant pagoda, a dab of burnt red
Well disposed on the edge of a gray hill;

I have lived for a long time this life
Of bare trees and chrysanthemums,
One road curving over a mountain top,
Words from my hand, crossing and descending;

Of what use this presence? To fill a space,
Balance a mountain? What stays
Is calligraphy; and these my words,
A blade of grass, the perfect line.

The Bus Driver

It's my safe world, moving through the dark,
Lozenge of warmth and light, a humming
Of soft conversation: weather and work,
Human voices, hushed and comforting.

I know my route: it is mapped and marked,
Road shines to the next turning,
I can see clearly everywhere
There's need to see; nothing beyond that

Worries me. New faces at the next corner,
They give me tokens, I get there

Slowly, change by shining change:
Everyone smiles at my silver arrivals.

And if the fare flips from numb fingers
Into a snowdrift, and they haven't the price
Of a ride, what is power given for,
If not forgiveness? The path's agleam

With light, and though the shell we move in
Jolts and rattles, I keep on driving
To the next stop. In my great ring
I go in the joy of constant arriving.

Road Kill

At night in rainless times small animals
Climb down and cross the road below the bridge
To drink. Each morning, a fresh corpse appears,
Small bodies with glazed eyes, raccoon, opossum,
Skunk; and once, a doe, her bristly sides still
Steaming warmth to the cool morning air.
She was removed, a potential traffic hazard,
But mostly they lie leathery and flat
Beneath the speeding cars. Necessity
And ignorance compel them, they keep coming,
Every night another one is smashed,
Most so small the driver doesn't notice.

Once in the Ozarks a pair of foxes darted
Into our lights. We hit the second one.
The female, probably, my husband said
As the corpse disappeared in darkness behind our car.
And our friend Stephen collided with a hawk
On an English country lane. *Not even airplanes
Escape his mighty weaponry*, we laughed—
Stephen, the eagle man with the flying car.

Corpses—comic, tragic, meaningless—
Litter our days and nights, like the ants
I finally spray in pure exasperation,
Their tiny bodies shriveling to dots
On the white counter top. Then I worry
Poison might get into our food. That evening,
Watching the endless lines of refugees
Crossing my TV screen, I wonder how
Any human could cause such suffering,
Remember them all—doe, foxes, ants—
How I explained it: they were in my way,
Wanted what was mine. I couldn't stop in time.

The Blessing of Snow

Beyond silence, icy silence,
There is nothing more to know,
No sound within or out:
We are alone with snow.
The silent deer keep shelter
In the woods, the gray squirrels
Sleep in the curve of their tails—

Until the lights of plows stab
The misty scrim of sky,
Scraping the road to ice,
Scattering salt and ash.

The street comes slowly to life:
Dark cars crawl down drives,
Exploding through the drifts,
Crackling the smooth ice;

Everyone has to get somewhere
Except for the woman watching,
Who, glad she has nowhere to go,

Stands in a niche of window,
Inscrutable as a medieval saint
Until the sun floods through.

What she sees and who sees her
Blessing the difficult travel
Of strangers to wherever
They have to go depends
Solely on the moment's light,
As do the gleaming branches
Of surrendering trees, made
Brilliant for an hour by their
Burdens of melting snow.

Photo by Ron McKoy

Sam Hamill

Biographical Sketch:

"I was born in 1943, orphaned during World War II, and grew up with a Utah farm family. My commitment to Zen and poetry as my essential path grew out of my interest in the San Francisco Renaissance and the Beat poets, especially Kenneth Rexroth. I come to poetry and Zen practice as a monk to his temple, and indeed the logo for Copper Canyon Press (where I have served as Founding Editor since 1972) is the Chinese/Japanese character for *poetry* and combines the word for *word* with the word for *temple*. Translating the great classical poets of China and Japan taught me how I wanted to live my life. Like those poets, I combine elements of Taoism and Confucianism with my Zen practice. Three decades ago, I built a little house in the woods near Port Townsend, Washington, and began mastering the arts of poverty, as Su Tung-p'o advised all poets to do. I taught in prisons for 14 years, and worked extensively with battered women and children."

Hamill has published about 40 books, including *Crossing the Yellow River: 300 Poems from the Chinese;* Basho's *Narrow Road to the Interior & Other Writings;* Issa's *The Spring of My Life;* Lao Tzu's *Tao Te Ching;* and 14 volumes of original poetry, including *Almost Paradise: New & Selected Poems & Translations* (Shambhala, 2005). In January, 2003, he founded Poets Against the War, and on March 5, 2003, delivered to congress 13,000 poems by 12,000 poets opposed to the Bush administrative attack on Iraq— the largest single-theme anthology of poetry in history.

Two Statements on Poetry and Zen:

From "The Long Apprentice" in *A Poet's Work* (Carnegie Mellon Press):

Giving up pride, giving up ambition, giving up the self, the poet moves closer to the Universal I of the poem. . . . Like Adrienne Rich, I dream of a common language. I do so knowing the first lesson of biology tells us that only diversity breeds health. I learn my lessons from women who aid battered women, from men in prisons for serious or innocuous 'victimless' crimes. When a man behind bars or a woman in a shelter responds to a poem, I suffer the sin of pride. I am grateful when a few lines I have written help another clarify significant perceptions. But the pride of authorship is a wall between the poet and the poem at hand.

I am a member of a tribe. I speak a particular regional dialect of a particular language. My inflections and my cadences are a signature as unique as any I ever signed on a check.

The self asserts itself sometimes, and at other times recedes. Making the poem, I suddenly remember Master Dogen: "We study the self to lose the self. Only when you forget yourself can you become one with all things."

*   *   *

Above heaven
big winds
    —Ryokan

Rising
> *December 24, 1998*

> *"No romance here, but a willingness to age*
> *and die at the speed of sound."* —Jim Harrison

It's time again not to push a metaphor too far,
but when solstice falls on frozen ground
and snow falls steadily on the water, islands
dissolving in the chalky distance,
and only a single crow in the sky,
I think of Yesenin at the doctor's,
finding the old woman whose legs were blue,
Akhmatova so solemn at the gates,
Tu Fu huddled over his charcoal stove,
trying to thaw his fingers enough
to hold his writing brush. Basho listened
in the silence to ice crack his rice jar.
The sky is slate white—a chalkboard
erased ten thousand times.

Winter solstice. Nothing inherently holy
in that, except the days grow longer now,
the cold a little less cold because it comes
on the wings of spring. It's Ramadan, Chanukah,
Kwanzaa and Christmas, and for a moment,
the missiles have been silenced. The world
is strangely still, trees black against the sky.
Hayden's alone in his little house in the eastern cold
as I am alone in mine, a continent away.
He writes of dialing 911:
"A helicopter ride would be fun."

Li Po looked up at a pale, thin moon
and raised his sake cup. Not much has changed.
Those who claim to know murder those
they call false prophets while science

improves their tools. There is death
in Jerusalem, frozen death among the homeless
all across the heartland. A president
is impeached, and the stock market rises.
Tibet is Chinese and the Makah want whales.

I got up from my *zafu* in the first gray light
and blew out the candle and went into the kitchen
and turned on the lights; I made a latte
and went outside and stood
shivering on the deck in the last of the dark,
remembering ten thousand dawns I watched
emerge from trees and mountains.

I remembered my wife rushing in from the garden,
"Let's go make love—the dragonflies are fucking!"
What man was I when I cleared this land
and built my hermitage? What man today?
I remembered the dogs I buried.
Slowly, a few snowy trees turned from dark to white.
This world is frost on an old man's breath,
memory rushing into memory.

Twenty years ago, on a warm midsummer night,
Gary Snyder got up on stage at the Town Tavern,
beer mug in hand, and recited "Ode to the West Wind"
in his indelibly lovely voice
to a boisterous, cheering crowd. It made me
feel alive at the speed of sound. Outside,
the same moon rose above the water
that Wang Wei watched rise over the river
a thousand years before. It was the same night.
It was the same poem.

The Orchid Flower

Just as I wonder
whether it's going to die,
the orchid blossoms

and I can't explain why it
moves my heart, why such pleasure

comes from one small bud
on a long spindly stem, one
blood red gold flower

opening at mid-summer,
tiny, perfect in its hour.

Even to a white-
haired craggy poet, it's
purely erotic,

pistil and stamen, pollen,
dew of the world, a spoonful

of earth, and water.
Erotic because there's death
at the heart of birth,

drama in those old sunrise
prisms in wet cedar boughs,

deepest mystery
in washing evening dishes
or teasing my wife,

who grows, yes, more beautiful
because one of us will die.

"True Illumination Is Habitude."

A perfect half-moon glistens
in the mist high over
the young bamboo.

The smoke-stained glass
I watch it through
makes a perfect halo

around it, as though
the moon were full. Below,
the trees are doubly dark

Where no breeze lifts
a leaf—nothing moves
that doesn't move

toward sleep. You move,
in another room,
into the Dreamtime world,

your hair flooding out
in soft waves
around your face.

The night is so
perfectly still
I can hear your every breath

above my beating heart.
The fire's long since
gone out.

Along by my lamp,
I read Rexroth's
Signature of All Things,

and once again,
like that swift bird
rising from its ashes,

the old ghost rises
from the wreckage of
this world

to touch my semi-
conscious life.
Poetry, Tu Fu says,

that will last
a thousand generations
comes only as

an unappreciated life
is passed.
I lay aside the book

and rub my weary eyes
just as Po Chu-i did
reading Yuan Chen

on his boat, by candlelight
a thousand years ago.
I sit motionless

in the motionless night
while mist
deepens

and the whole house
cools,
I listen to your breath

and measure it against
the slow, insistent tolling
of our flesh.

After a Winter of Grieving

> *Before I traveled my road I was my road.*
> *—Antonio Porchia*
> *No road leads the way.*
> *The road follows behind.*
> *—Takamura Kotaro*

With the moon so bright,
I could not sleep, the garden
glowing in cold white light.

I rose, dressed, and went out
to the deck to sit in the cold and think.

The April moon was full and high,
almost big enough to burst,
haloed by a ring of sparkling light
and a few bright stars.

The garden Buddha, a pretty boy,
wore an apron of moss.

The old Moon Watching Pavilion,
where I watched this moon with my daughter
nearly thirty years ago,
rots under the katsura tree.

I watched the first gray light begin to seep
through the trees before
the first robin arrived. Each gain,
each loss, had a name I could not speak.

Denise called this, "A kind
of Paradise," this logged-off scrappy land
I came to thirty years ago,
impoverished by my needs.

Paradise is a sometime thing,
wherever one might make it—
a river of stones, bamboo, a foreign tree,
building a home alone—

and this same old moon,
eternally new
in geologic time.

The road to *Kage-an* is gone.
Don't ask me where I've been.
The road out is the road in.

William Heyen

Biographical Sketch

photo by Bud Meade

280' behind his home in Brockport, New York, William Heyen has an 8' x 12' cabin where, as his friend William Stafford once wrote, he "invites" as many poems in as will join him. Within bushes, rain, trees, birdsong, snow, this hermitage without doorbell or phone or television, has in ineffable ways helped form Heyen's books—*Long Island Light, Erika: Poems of the Holocaust, Ribbons: The Gulf War, Crazy Horse in Stillness, Shoah Train*, and the nature books *Pterodactyl Rose* and *The Rope* among them. Writing this paragraph in the third person, trying in his increasingly floating world to remember something rock-solid from thirty-five years of teaching, he knows he is still a work-in-progress, but now he is sixty-three, sitting in his cabin easy chair, and several things have occurred to him at once: how Robert Frost became "overtired" of the great harvest he himself desired; how Lucien Stryk despised "the hateful evidence of our will to impress"; how Heyen's now deceased father and older brother built this place for him (despite contentions along the way); how Joyce Carol Oates once said to him, "Just do it"; how there are two contradictory sayings about playing a strong game of poker: 1) don't fall in love with your cards, and 2) scared cards never win; how Richard Hugo said that semi-colons are ugly. This old poem of mine about this place: "Under my cabin, / field mice, and China." -W. H.

Zen Statement

I've had fun over the years asking kids, "What's the difference between a duck?" This joke, or koanic riddle, makes them laugh, stumps them, but makes the logicians among them ask, of course, "Between a duck and what?" The answer, I tell them, is "One leg is both the same."

The other morning I was playing with three-year-old grandson Nick. For the first time, it occurred to me to ask him, "Nick, what's the difference between a duck?" Immediately, in less than half a second he shouted, "Lollipop." We hadn't been talking about candy, hadn't been sucking on lollipops. This was the verbal equivalent of the moment in Eugen Herrigel's classic *Zen in the Art of Archery* when the Master tells Eugen how a child lets go of an adult finger: "There is not the slightest jerk. Do you know why? Because a child doesn't think: I will now let go of the finger in order to grasp this other thing." Our words, our actions should open "like the skin of a ripe fruit," the Master says.

I know this poetry when I read it. It does not, in fact, tell me that it *is* poetry, so unselfconscious is it, so natural. It does not lurch into concept or calculation, is not content within an inherited state of mind, of being. Its perspective, its seeing-through-to, is vast. It does not lurch. It is uncomplicated, but fathomless. It is song not available to my intelligence, is refracted by any pressure of thought, is not negotiable in any marketplace of hard currency. It is at the same time receptive to any well-meaning companion who will breathe its rhythms and sounds. It will not resist or repel us, but will absorb us entire while we are within it. Sadaharu Oh's batting instructor told him that he must see with the eye in his hip. Can you see him, his one-legged lefty stance at the American plate, that eye as big as the stadium, as the moon, the Milky Way, as huge as a lollipop?

Sake Gold

(Anthony Piccione 1939-2001)

1.
passing through passing
clouds—cherry pits & squirrel shit
in my birdbath

2.
took a chance ran to
my cabin through lightning—odds
against satori

3.
poison ivy takes my
hermitage three leaves by
tendrils at a time

4.
morning rain within
this cabin—I need candlelight
to praise such gloom

5.
the spirit ocean—
first wash ourselves before
entering the great bath

6.
infusions those last days—
sunshine birdcall voices
of loved ones *chemo*

7.
fisheyes in rice wine
my memory swims in sake—
too much to drink

8.
I'm half envious
of my dead friend—he's got death
over & done with

9.
the "oldest man in Japan"—
four slivers of bone
& his reflection

10.
cherryglint starlight
surfeit of beauty—this wind
a hearse in the leaves

11.
will you sip these haiku—
bottle of sake
rattlesnake coiled inside

12.
smell the ripe sushi
my dead refrigerator's
raspberry liquor

13.
say the four great fears
of the Japanese—*earthquake*
thunder fire father

14.
bumper sticker—
Jesus saves / Buddha invests—we trust
which or what bank

15.
from our climbing sticks
bells seek the chiming center
of the universe

16.
latrines on Fuji—
stench of ten thousand climbers
every summer night

17.
engagement diamond—
crystalline dream Fuji as
translucent starlight

18.
cherry blossoms our
human hearts—Hiroshima
summer Pearl Harbor

19.
which cherry petal
counts others as it descends—
such fun to catch you

20.
open-mouthed dreaming
until dragonfly drills sheen
into my eyetongue

21.
we'll brush goldenrod
as we pass—star profusion
evening moon pollen

22.
gohan   furo   futon—
food   bath   bed—lazy haiku
lets others work

23.
all nothing nothing
all—jackhammer hammering
sparrow vacuum call

24.
farewell friend until
Tao knows when until *your* last
tongue of templebell

25.
drink for a dead poet—
from now forward goldflakes
flowing in our blood

26.
our priest claps twice
to summon the gods—then thunder
& cherry blossoms

27.
crematorium—
winter's porcelain light a cry
from my friend's urn

28.
sumo wrestler—
quarter ton of eel & kelp spirit
lunges upward

Words

Wind in the fur of living buffalo dead
ten thousand years ago. Imagining one,
trying to imagine him: It's spring,
this bull's fur patched, he's shedding,
his longest hairs ruffle, he's grazing,
head down, but watchful for wolves....
Yes, gusts lift patches of fur on his neck,
flies lift from grasses, sunflowers
brush his flank crusted with mud,
sun clots in the thickest tufts of fur.
Winter is elsewhere in memory, this
is what is, grass for its mouth,
invisible odors of flowers, air ruffling fur
with the promise of sustenance over
the long, slow, instinctual migration.
& now night falls. & now Time
cannot preserve the beast's fur, or ours,
& now words are fur shed
in prairie spring ten thousand years before.

Where

Cabin morning, probes of wind after rain,
western New York State, mid-September,
six weeks left of my fifties,
broad-leaf milkweed in margins around me,
ash & silver maple dripping, wild roses
reaching late new growth toward my door,
honeysuckle & red osier framing my windows,

sprouts of elm from rotted stumps, their
toothed yellowgreen leaves last of their kind
on these remnant acres into which
I now retire. No one will miss or need me

in those classrooms where, as years passed,
I distrusted what I'd once professed.
I began to grow so quiet I became

the books I read, those voices of the dead
who seem more prescient than the living,
who are often—can this be forgiven me?—
my true soul-mates. Whoever you are in my future,
we'll meet in sounds, in indentations
of silver maple leaves, in the whistles of cardinals
& these ash thinning in wind, or nowhere.

Jane Hirshfield

Biographical Sketch

Jane Hirshfield was born in 1953 and raised in New York City. Her interest in Japanese literature and a Buddhist worldview developed early: her first purchased book, at age eight, was a collection of Japanese haiku. She received zazen instruction in tenth grade, as part of a high school fieldtrip, and began sitting on her own while at Princeton University while also taking classes in Japanese and Chinese literature in translation. "I was twenty-one when I began to study Zen—it was what I did instead of graduate school." In 1974, she became a fulltime student at the San Francisco Zen Center, which included eight years of study, three of monastic practice at their Tassajara Center where Philip Whalen was a fellow student and became head monk. She received lay ordination in Soto Zen in 1979.

Her most recent poetry collection, *Given Salt* (HarperCollins 2001) was a finalist in the National Book Critics Circle Award and winner of the Bay Area Book Reviewers Award. Her previous collections include: *The Lives of the Heart* (HarperCollins 1997), *The October Palace* (HarperCollins 1994), and *Of Gravity & Angels* (Wesleyan 1988). She edited and co-translated *The Ink Dark Moon: Poems by Komachi and Shikiu, Women of the Ancient Court of Japan* (Vintage Classic 1990). Her collection of essays *Nine Gates: Entering the Mind of Poetry* (HarperCollins 1997) is an important study of Zen and poetry.

In Lieu of a Zen Statement:
From *Fooling with Words: A Celebration of Poets and Their Craft*
(HarperCollins 1999)

Bill Moyers: *What can you say about your own experience of Zen—
I mean, insofar as it influences your writing?*

Jane Hirshfield: The specific meditation practice is one of developing attentiveness to this moment, at first by settling your awareness within the breath while keeping your body centered and alert. You aren't doing anything but offering up your attention, yet somehow that "doing nothing" allows mind, body, emotion, the rain on the roof, to come together and reveal themselves. It's as if you were to sit very quietly in the woods: after a while, the animals begin to emerge, and you see the full amplitude of life that is in fact already there. The intention is to live your whole life in that kind of awareness. To be translucently awake—which should be simple, but somehow is quite hard—instead of living in a haze of distraction, hope, and fear, as we usually do. And you don't want to come to this state only in meditation: you want to be awake when you sand a floor or speak in a meeting or tie up the newspapers for recycling.

I try to be awake when I write a poem, and I think that Zen training showed me a way to do that. The combination of focused awareness and open permeability that goes into writing poetry is very similar to meditative mind, but the difference is that when I write, I am leaning my attention and my intention a little more into the realm of language, thought, and expression. Zen pretty much comes down to three things—everything changes; everything is connected; pay attention. It is simply a path toward entering your life more fully, a way of knowing the taste of your tongue in your own mouth. The path of poetry and shaped words is much the same, I think—each increases what we can know of human experience.

The Dead Do Not Want Us Dead

The dead do not want us dead;
such petty errors are left for the living.
Nor do they want our mourning.
No gift to them—not rage, not weeping.
Return one of them, any one of them, to the earth,
and look: such foolish skipping,
such telling of bad jokes, such feasting!
Even a cucumber, even a single anise seed: feasting.

September 15, 2001

The Monk Stood Beside a Wheelbarrow

The monk stood beside a wheelbarrow, weeping

God or Buddha nowhere to be seen—
these tears were fully human,
bitter, broken,
falling onto the wheelbarrow's rusty side.

They gathered at its bottom,
where the metal drank them in to make more rust.

You cannot know what you do in this life, what you have done.

The monk stood weeping.
I knew I also had a place on this hard earth.

To Judgement: An Assay

You change a life
as eating an artichoke changes the taste
of whatever is eaten after.
Yet you are not an artichoke, not a piano or cat—
not objectively present at all—
and what of you a cat possesses is essential but narrow:
to know if the distance between two things can be leapt.
The piano, that good servant,
has none of you in her at all, she lends herself
to what asks; this has been my ambition as well.
Yet a person who has you is like an iron spigot
whose water comes from far-off mountain springs.
Inexhaustible, your confident pronouncements flow,
coldly delicious.
For if judgement hurts the teeth, it doesn't mind,
not judgement. Teeth pass. Pain passes.
Judgement decrees what remains—
the serene judgementts of evolution or the judgement
of a boy-king entering Persia: "Burn it," he says,
and it burns. And if a small tear swells the corner
of one eye, it is only the smoke, it is no more to him than a beetle
fleeing the flames of the village with her six-legged children.
The biologist Haldane—in one of his tenderer moments—
judged beetles especially loved by God,
"because He had made so many." For judgement can be tender:
I have seen you carry a fate to its end as softly as a retriever
carries the quail. Yet however much
I admire you at such moments, I cannot love you:
you are too much in me, weighing without pity your own worth.
When I have erased you from me entirely,
disrobed of your measuring adjectives,
stripped from my shoulders and hips each of your nouns,
when the world is horsefly, coal barge, and dawn the color of
        winter butter—
not *beautiful*, not *cold*, only the color of butter—

then perhaps I will love you. Helpless to not.
As a newborn wolf is helpless: no choice but drink the wolf milk,
and find it sweet.

It Was Like This: You Were Happy

It was like this:
you were happy, then you were sad,
then happy again, then not.

It went on.
You were innocent or you were guilty.
Actions were taken, or not.

At times you spoke, at other times you were silent.
Mostly, it seems you were silent—what could you say?

Now it is almost over.

Like a lover, your life bends down and kisses your life.

It does this not in forgiveness—
between you, there is nothing to forgive—
but with the simple nod of a baker at the moment
he sees the bread is finished with transformation.

Eating, too, is a thing now only for others.

It doesn't matter what they will make of you
or your days: they will be wrong,
they will miss the wrong woman, miss the wrong man,
all the stories they tell will be tales of their own invention.

Your story was this: you were happy, then your were sad,
you slept, you awakened.
Sometimes you ate roasted chestnuts, sometimes persimmons.

Holly Hughes

Biographical Sketch

Holly Hughes lives in a log cabin built in the 1930s in Indianola, Washington, near the shores of Puget Sound. A native of Minnesota, she headed northwest to Alaska after college to make money for graduate school and was seduced by the sea. She has spent the last twenty-six summers on the waters of Alaska working on boats in a variety of capacities, from deckhand/cook on a salmon gillnetter to mate on a research vessel to skipper of a sixty-five-foot schooner. During the winter, she teaches a variety of writing classes at Edmonds Community College and co-directs the college's Convergence Writers Series program. She began a Vipassana Buddhist practice just seven years ago, and suspects that all those seasons working on the water were good preparation for meditation.

Holly Hughes' poems have appeared or are forthcoming in *The Midwest Quarterly, Alaska Quarterly Review, americas review, Pontoon, The Hedgebrook Journal,* and two anthologies: *Salt in Our Veins,* and *Fish in the Freezer.* Her essays have appeared in *Crosscurrents* and the anthology *Steady As She Goes: Women's Adventures at Sea.* An alumna of Hedgebrook, a retreat for women writers on Whidbey Island, she is currently enrolled in the Rainier Writing Workshop M.F.A Program at Pacific Lutheran University.

Statement about Zen Practice

My opportunity to experience Zen practice came several summers ago while co-leading a kayak/meditation trip in Southeast Alaska with Zen practitioner Kurt Hoelting, of *Inside Passages*. We spent a week kayaking among humpback whales, paddling in silence, and practicing sitting and walking meditation ashore at our campsites. This practice of silence deepened my experience of Alaska and strengthened my connection to Buddhism as well. As a student in the *Vipassana* tradition for seven years now, I have watched as this practice found its way into my poems. For me, the two are now inextricably intertwined.

For the past seven years, I have begun most mornings in darkness, lighting a candle, sitting on my round black cushion, watching my breath. After sitting I move to my desk to write, following the same impulses that guide my sitting: notice what's in front of me, the life out my window, breathe, pay attention to my body. Writing with intention slowly began to shape how I write, how I approach the day, my poems, my life. When I can't write anything else, I can always write my morning poem and I've came to rely on this practice as a way to keep writing, go deeper. I've learned there is little separation between the two practices, except the obvious difference in where I am sitting. One feeds the other; both move me out of my mind and into my heart and therefore, more deeply into the world. Both are as essential to my life as breathing. The poems here are all morning poems from a chapbook called *Heart & Mind*, published by Flying Squirrel Press in 2002, and reflect teachings found within the *Vipassana* tradition. A deep bow of gratitude to my *Vipassana* teachers: Jack Kornfield, Sharon Salzburg, Debra Chamberlin, Sandy Boucher.

At the Teahouse, 6 am

Sunrise at the octagonal hut;
beyond, where two decks meet,
a lizard does pushups in the sun.
I see the green, chattering world
through the window, I see
my image in the window.
Both are present; are both true?
A bee enters the hut, buzzes
insistently against the window,
but the window won't yield
to his wishes. I want to
show him the open door,
say *this world through the glass
is only an illusion* but I don't.
How long will he hurl himself
against the dusty glass? How long
will we believe we are not free?

At the Teahouse, 7 am

Sitting until the sun rises
over the oak studded hill.
7 am and already hot
in this octagonal teahouse,
picture of the Buddha
tattered, fixed by rusty tacks,
Om mani padne om fading.
I sit with my skittish heart
ask it to want what it has,
to give up what is not,
as it circles happiness
like a hungry dog, wary.

On the way down the footpath,
five deer. They look at me
calmly in that other way,
chew sideways the acorns
they've snuffled out from
drying oak leaves, ears
rotating like semaphores.
The two youngest are most
curious. They look at me
as if wanting more, not sure
why I can't give it, boundaries
between beings not yet
drawn in their world.
May all beings be happy,
I say to them. *May all*
Beings be free. Soon
may I join this sun-mottled,
acorn-crunching, stilt-
legged, skittery world.

Invitation to the Cricket

A cricket calls while I am sitting, lost
in no-thought, calls its lisping chirrup,
its leg-pulsing, wing-quivering song,
calls me back to this world and
I swim up, happy to be plumbed
back by this minute ambassador of
summer nights, when I slept with
only a sheet, June bugs sequining
the screen door, and the cricket
somehow inside, though I never
knew exactly where, only that he
sang each evening, running
his quiet bow along crisp
tendoned strings. Yesterday

I heard a Tibetan lama describe
a saint's aversion to bathing
as a perfect union of elegance and
outrageousness, something we all
he says, are seeking. I get up
from my cushion and open
the door, invite a cricket in.

Mind Wanting More

Only a beige slat of sun
above the horizon, like a shade pulled
not quite down.   Otherwise,
clouds. Sea rippled here and
there. Birds reluctant to fly.
The mind wants a shaft of sun to
stir the grey porridge of clouds,
an osprey to stitch sea to sky
with its barred wings, some dramatic
music: a symphony, perhaps
a Chinese gong.

But the mind always
wants more than it has—
one more bright day of sun,
one more clear night in bed
with the moon; one more hour
to get the words right; one
more chance for the heart in hiding
to emerge from its thicket
in dried grasses—as if this quiet day
with its tentative light weren't enough,
as if joy weren't strewn all around.

Mary Sue Koeppel

Biographical Sketch

Mary Sue Koeppel was born at home in a tiny, blue-collar town in north central Wisconsin. "As a child growing up, my favorite image was of the sun setting into deep, blue snow. My father owned a small store and construction business whose purpose, he believed, was not financial gain but social service; my mother served as an elementary school teacher and principal. From them, I learned to serve others and the excitement of books and ideas."

For sixteen years, she was a devote Catholic nun, taking vows and teaching in high schools. Later, she left the convent, taught in a technical college, married, and moved to Florida. For the last eleven years, she has sat with a Zen Buddhist monk. Just this last spring, the Mountain Sky Zendo where she sometimes sits was formally dedicated by Eido T. Shimano, abbot of Dai Bosatsu Zendo in upstate New York.

Koeppel teaches composition courses and creative writing at Florida Community College at Jacksonville. Also, for the past 16 years she has been the editor of *Kalliope*, a national journal of women's literature and art. Among her teaching honors are the Florida Association of Community Colleges' Red Schoolhouse Florida Professor of the Year Award and the 2002 Cultural Council of Greater Jacksonville Educator of the Year Award.

Koeppel workshops with visually impaired women at the Cummer Museum of Art & Gardens and has co-edited a book of the women's writings: *Women of Vision, an Experience in Seeing by the Visually Impaired.* Through grants, she has edited and published two books of children's and teens' writings which are given free to children in homeless shelters.

Her own books include *In the Library of Silences—Poems of Loss* (Rhiannon Press, 2001) and *Writing Strategies—Plus Collaboration* (Pearson, 4th ed. 2004).

Zen Statement

I was a Catholic nun for sixteen years before I left the convent in search of a deeper context to meaning than Catholicism. That search brought me to Buddhism, first through reading and then by working with a Zen Buddhist monk in Jacksonville, Florida.

In rereading T. S. Eliot last week, I was amazed that the emotional reactions I had when I first found his words in college were still there all these years later. Perhaps Eliot was my first introduction to Buddhism, (the way a good Catholic girl meets new ideas in college). Eliot and my brother's death the summer of his first year of college taught me much about Zen

My writing is part of my searching to get a deeper understanding of the truths of Zen. Sometimes I see my poetry as the voice of an ex-Catholic nun chanting, like a Zen Buddhist, in her limited vocabulary.

One can be a Buddhist-Jesuit priest. That, to me, is one of the glories of American Zen. We can heighten our experience of the moment, not by denigrating the religions we first understood, but by charging them with Zen.

People ask, "What are you doing about your mysticism?" I don't experience mysticism. But I have a deep belief in the universal oneness of all. I believe that living or dead, I belong to the great ALL, the great wholeness in this moment. In this I find the ability to let go. After all, what is so important to hang onto, if all is part of who we all are now? In that is peace, gentle strength, deep comfort, and in fact, wholeness. This awareness is what I try to give to my poetry.

Meditation

> Wise men do not grieve
> having discarded sorrow.
> *Dhammapada*

Sorrow is to be discarded,
not thrown out like garbage,
not fingered or sorted
or given to less fortunate,
but discarded like old cells,
like flakes of skin in the shower,
discarded like long hair
wound through a pointed comb.

A part that is not a part
any more is not grieved.
Wise ones neither mourn,
nor weep, nor squint in pain,
but sit in sacred stillness.
Peace is the quiet discarding.

While the Wolf Walks the Edge of the Woods

someone, turning in sleep
and asking, who,
and not expecting an answer
but turning again and
hearing the bell clap
knows it is early, but
the sangha meets before
sun or light or warmth
The nuns kowtow
to the floor and one
wonders if they bow

to Buddha or the light
beginning to streak
in the bamboo curtain
When the light reaches
the eyelids, the sight
says open and the eye
sees the grass bending
against the palmetto
and the palmetto bending
with the robin singing
and the robin bending
to the northeaster and
the whole sangha just
chanting to the rhythm
of the gong   Enough
it is enough   it is

Begin with the Heron and the Bat

All these years
I've slept,
waking sometimes
for a millisecond
to see
the blue heron
                stand on one leg
or the Harley
                on the kick stand.

All these years
I've prayed
for sight
for sleeplessness
so the bat
flying in the door
at dusk

is no stranger
but a welcome bedmate.

All these years
I've prayed,
and now the sleeplessness
and the blue heron
                above the pond
welcome the bat
who skims the skein of light
                dropping over the water
And the water
                drops over me
as the air says,
                holy, holy, holy.

The red fox
                fights the wild turkey
while the cat
                mews from a window.
When the earth's shadow
                eclipses the moon,
the dark pond
                turns black,
the turkey feathers
                hold water and sink.

    There the pond
                says glory,
the light
                sings hail,
and the bushes
                whisper hush.

9 PM Summer

Daylight fades, like the close of a long stemmed tiger lily
wide open for just the day, then withering but holding
its stain: red dye for sky, clear pond, pines, and elms.

Day fades. A mallard floats into the stippled pond.
Ripples ring two fish leaping where the dam flings
water into electricity; the foam turns red.

Night settles into the sky, the pond, the quiet fishermen.
When a car pulls up, radio blaring, no one says, "Sh."
The radio quits, a door slams. One more person stands quiet.

A black Lab noses next to the fishermen, lies, head on paws,
stares at the place where wind ripples the black pond.
One light in the A-frame across the water reflects silence.

Tomorrow the loons and doves will call at 4 AM.
Pike and walleye will surface for flies.
The sun will rise and dye sky and pond again. In reverse.

Mark S. Kuhar

Biographical Sketch

Mark S. Kuhar was born in 1958 in Cleveland, Ohio, and raised in rural Hinckley Township, surrounded by farms, forest and unfavorable roads. He currently lives in Medina, Ohio, with his wife and three children. He attended Ohio University, graduating in 1980 with a degree in English/Creative Writing. His poetry is influenced by the Beats, the work of the "mimeo revolution" poets of the 1960s, as well as poets and writers of various mystic traditions. His work has appeared in *Whiskey Island, Centerlight, The American Srbobran, The City, Tin Lustre Mobile, Ohio On-Line, Big Bridge, Sidereality, American Motor Thought, Litvert, Cool Cleveland, Getunderground* and *Northern Ohio Live*, as well as in the anthologies: *An Eye for an Eye Makes the Whole World Blind: Poets on 9/11* (Regent Press), *The Long March of Cleveland, Ornamental Iron* and *Mac's Turns a New Trick* (Green Panda Press) and *The LitKicks Book*.

His chapbook, *acrobats in catapult twist* was published in June 2003 by Seven Beers and a Hedgehog Press, Pepper Pike, Ohio, and his poems have been published by 24th St. Irregular Press, Sacramento, Calif., as part of the "Poems-for-All"series of mini-books. He has read his work on National Public Radio' and is the co-host of the deep cleveland poetry hour, a live monthly spoken-word event. He is also the proprietor of the publishing, entertainment and education group deep cleveland llc, **http://www.deepcleveland.com** which includes, among other projects, deep cleveland press, a small-press publishing company, and *deep cleveland junkmail oracle*, a literary e-zine dedicated to the spirit of legendary cleveland outlaw poet, artist & underground publisher d.a levy. He is the editor of *Ohio Writer Magazine.*

Statement: Zen Spirit

american zen spirit is a state of being wherein one views american life with beautiful detachment, with no resistance to vapid cultural onslaught, advertising cluster bombs, or electronic overload, a place where we seek to connect & discover a oneness with everything, a mutual interconnectedness open in free streams & uninterrupted perception, where satori can be reaped in miscellaneous moments of suburban hum. america zen congeals when we cultivate an inner laughter that only naturally follows from the absurdity of everyday life, when every action and reaction becomes an art of pure consciousness. the poetry that evolves from this state of being is subconscious in nature, spontaneous in construction, and ecstatic in expression—a holy refrain of the soul. & everything i/you/we know right now, will change, & the only thing that matters is the postcard we write ourselves from the dharma fields.

all holyroadz home

they're tearing up the street
just outside my door
front end loader crashes concrete
jackhammer pounds
lout in hard hat
screams about rebar & ready mix
while here inside
i light sandlewood incense
rake the zen garden
scribble mad pomes
to the universe
exhale sweet smoke
building a soul from scratch
seeking all holyroadz home

on the galloping cusp of the new now

in front of the building where the florist
arranges flats of yellow marigolds in rows
it's the new now, inside the gas station
a third-shift dock worker buys a six-pack
it's the new now, police cars lined up
in front of a sidestreet house
with lights flashing, no sirens wailing
it's the new now in back of the brick church
where the priest throws bread crumbs to birds
it's the new now in front of the tailor shop,
the owner hoses off the sidewalk as a spray
of droplets rainbows through sunned air,
the apartment building on the corner with
stark balconies, clothes out to dry, tricycles
& bikes leaning against sad walls, lawn chairs
it's the new now there, people moving inside
a delivery truck driver navigates the street curb

in the new now, turning a hard concrete corner
it's the new now, old lady with babushka walking
up the sidewalk, pulling a metal grocery cart
two children tripping & laughing in sweet bliss
in the barbershop magazines read in the new now
hair cut in the new now, i'm sitting on a stone bench
near a garden that's a clash of color, powdery red smells
a thousand-year-old bohdisattva in black boots,
a mediterranean cave mystic with blue eyes
a walking desert dervish monk on pilgrimmage
on the galloping cusp of the new now
this is the morning of the four fire winds
this is the moment that remains here forever

suburban buddha, coffeehouse christ

i can't be contained in this tiny body
not a body, but pure consciousness
on these streets in quiet houses buddha sits
buddha mows lawns, buddha rakes leaves
buddha drinks beer in calm yards, buddha cleans
buddha plays solitaire in the dark,
rising from pristine slumber i can't be contained
can't be held down here, can't be limited
to the miniscule things of this small place
suburban buddha waits holding fast

i can't be contained in this town, in this body,
this consciousness, slouching along lamplit streets
the windows of stores blank nobody nothing
i vanish into the sanctuary of a coffeehouse
where christ drinks freshbrew, packets of sugar
scattered on wooden tables, christ reads a magazine,
stares at baked offerings, smiling christ
pervades beating hearts standing in line
waiting for a holy decaf & latte liturgy

i can't be contained in the walls of this place
coffeehouse christ sits calmly waiting

i sit down,
i walk home in the beautiful arms of day

on the death of philip whalen

there is no such thing
as death, you can't
kill something that
has no beginning or
end, on some triangle
mountaintop sitting
crosslegged, buddha
belly pointed east,
yr brothers welcome
you, philip, & the dance
of clouds over vast
canyons makes a sound
that only you can hear

you can't blow up the buddha

the taliban blew up the buddha
cliff carvings hundreds of feet
tall, etched in the mountain stone
they said it was the worship of idols,
& an affront to islam, tall buddha
bas relief rock commemorations
thousands of years old, blasted
into rubble & cosmic dust, but
what the taliban didn't know is
you can't blow up the buddha
he's already blown (pure) sky high

Mac Lojowsky

Photo by Bernadette Esposito

Biographical Sketch

Mac Lojowsky was born in Cleveland, Ohio, December 12, 1977. "I grew up on a lake named Erie with two sisters and a cat named Leroy. Studied politics and poetry at Kent State University, and graduated the Evergreen State College in poetry and politics." He worked for awhile as a backcountry ranger with Alaska State Parks, then hitchhiked, boated, and backpacked around lots of the far North Country. He is currently working as a house carpenter and living below the Sespe Mountains in Ojai, California.

Zen Statement

Zen Poetry. An empty boat sailing a hooked halibut on the Skelikof Strait, a trail closed by the Devil's Club, West 117th Street broken schoolhouse windows, lakes without name, lakes named "Danger-No Swimming!" sinking salt lakes, Mecca, California, Tenino, Washington, Lebenon, Ohio, my back yard, your backyard, six-shooters that don't shoot no more, cold mountains, hot mountains, graffiti at the Arctic Circle, a whiskey bottle passed round a Colorado campfire, a stew pot passed round a thanksgiving table.

It ain't in no Presidential funeral or dead chump speech, ain't in no new *New Yorker* magazine, won't find it in any MFA classroom or any CEO boardroom, it don't make Headline News and isn't considered in the latest Gallop Poll—it puts sugar into the gas tanks of search engines, gets harassed by policemen disguised as poets, it's not attached to any political party, has no campaign funds to contribute and won't be awarded any reconstruction contracts anytime soon. *Vanity Fair* will not come knocking to find it and George W. Bush has never heard of it.

Zen Poetry. Who am I to say anything? The sun rises in the East, sets in the West. Occasionally gets eclipsed by the Moon.

Horizon

Circled by a circle,
shines across broken night—
full moon on the rise.

Even fir-peaked arrows
point in prayer;
This moon!

On the Sixth Day of the War

In town, the news grows
worse and worse—
bombs falling on Afghanistan,
anthrax in New Jersey,
California bridges that might blow up.

On this here mountain,
the news stays the same—
water flows down stream,
birds sing in manzanita
sage brush bows to wind.

In the Cage of Doves

How long since I sat last?
Two, maybe three years,
except for that one time drunk
on the Lowell River—
but I've been busy.

You know how it goes;
long nights from long days,
long months from long weeks.

At some point,
you find yourself somewhere.

I find myself thinning a pepper tree
above an old farmhouse
in Southern California.

Next to the house sits a dove coop—
constant call of "coo-coo, woo-woo"
through the chainsaw's growl.

On break, I walk over to the cage.

Locked in this cage
sits a stone statue of Buddha
below ten white doves.

The Buddha is buried neck deep in shit.

I go inside the cage,
bow to Buddha,
dove shits on my head.

This is far from Enlightenment,
it is closer to a lesson
that I have not learned.

Big Fort Island Buddha

I.
Word comes in this afternoon
I have seven days.
After that: two plane rides,
a thirteen hour boat
and many miles of city road
to take me back.

Tonight I consider;
What if I don't leave
and simply wander off
into the bush?

I could set up a small shack
near a fresh spring,
chop wood when the cold comes,
eat berries when the warm sun shines.

I could let my hair grow strange,
bathe only under a full moon,
write poems on the bark
of old spruce trees.

Nobody would know where I went
and eventually figure me gone.
My friends and lovers would move on
and so would I.

I would swim with the salmon,
howl with the wind
and burn like fire
through the lonely nights.

II.
Just off the southeast corner of Shuyak
there sits an old homestead
on a small island
named Big Fort.

About ten years ago
the old man out there died.
His wife moved to Kodiak,
leaving a furnished log cabin,
a half-sunken freighter
and a horse.

Even though at every low tide
Big Fort Island connects to Shuyak Island,
that horse never left—
He forgot his name
and still roams there today.

Nobody really knows how he has survived
the long dark winters alone,
winters that starve deer,
put bears to sleep.

In defiance to both logic
and probability, that horse
continues to live
alone and away by choice.

III.
Despite my words,
seven days from now,
when that state float plane lands,
I will leave with it.

I will return to a land crowded
with more people
and less water.

Again, I will strap on
my leather carpenter's bags
and allow some boss
to ride my hours.

"Is that wall plumb?"
"Pick up more two-by-fours."
"Hurry up!"

For this, I will get a paycheck
to trade for unpaid bills
and an afterwork body too torn
to do anything more
than eat and sleep.

I would like to believe
that horse and I
are the same
but it wouldn't be true.

Ray McNiece

Biographical Sketch

"I wasborn in Appalachia, raised on the banks of the Ohio in the summers, and the shores of Lake Erie in the winters...Chagrin River rapids...sitting on sun-baked boulder amid stones arranged when the last ice age melted away, I breathe once molten igneous rock and pollen into empty belly bowl, breathe out susurrating fugue of current and tree bank reflection swirling surface dimpled by small mouth bass swallowing life fallen.

"As reminiscences surface, I follow the flow to hemlocked Gullybrook where I waded through father-loss Bardo shadow until finding, by way of Lynn Robinson's World of Books, the Tao. I heeded Lao Tsu, no longer dwelling on the morbidity but embracing the immediacy of life-death. The Readiness is all. I hiked with Basho, Thoreau, Snyder awake to the dharma's tributaries: Chaung Tsu's parables, Wang Wei's Ch'an lyrics, Basho's haibun and Thoreau's transcendental sojourns, following that creek to storm-pipe drain, freeway roar above, where I hitched a ride with Kerouac to East Coast big city kicks.

"Along the way I studied with a varied *sangha* of elders, teachers and children: learning to be at home in the wild from Grandma Zelma, Appalachian root woman who glowed with Methodist love and awareness,studying Chinese poetics with Julia Lin and translating Li Po, Tu Fu and Po-Chu-I, and playing verbal games with kids. In the bright lights of Boston's stages, inspired by Dad's vaudeville dreams, I practiced breath and body expression through solo shows of monologues and songs. *Dis–Voices from a Shelter* yoked art with compassion dharma, expanded to the social engagement of *Us/Versus*.

"Later I met Tadashi Kondo on a ginko, carrying on the haiku hikes while in residence at the Cuyahoga Valley National Park, those poems gathered in *wet sand raven tracks*. Always a rambler, I took the frozen freeway to the deep south for another residency in the house where Jack wrote *Dharma Bums*. The journey came full circle from mystery of father's death while collaborating with Ray Bobgan for Cleveland Public Theater on the *Tibetan Book of the Dead* adaptation, *Blue Sky Transmission,* breathed out."

Ray McNiece is the author of five books of poems: *Dis— Voices from a Shelter, The Bone-Orchard Conga, The Road that Carried Me Here*, *wet sand raven tracks* and *Song that Fathoms Home*. He created two poetry musicals, *Mouth Music* and *Rustbowl Hootenanny* and served as collaborating author for *Blue Sky Transmission, A Tibetan Book of the Dead.*

Zen Statment

But back to the clear trickle, oriole whistle, sun shaft through hemlock dusk Gullybrook. The whole of the place sounded the way Wang Wei spoke, *the rising moon startles the mountain birds/ their song inside the steam*; the way Heraclitus spoke, *you can't step in the same stream twice*; the way Isaiah spoke, *the water wears the stone and the stone wears away*; the way Hopkins spoke, *for rose-moles all in stipple upon trout that swim*; the way the Tao itself spoke, *the way that can be spoken is not the true way*. For poetry in general and haiku in particular always speak on the edge of the unutterable. Haiku cannot capture that swirl on the stream. Though the poet can hold up the moss covered stone glistening cold. Sit on this bank long enough and that stone will wear down to sand through mortal hands. But who can sit that long? And that's the point of haiku's poignancy. We live moment-to-moment, movement-by-movement. Haiku blossom from the realm of the space-time continuum, which is why they are written in the present tense. They speak from the eternal now grounded in natural and fragile particulars, the nexus of precise focus on an event unfolding in time, exact without being statistical, measured not in meters and hours but by hand spans, leaf falls and warbler inflections. And there is no space and no time. That's a leap for Americans deifying science, let alone the Christian Right. And yet this Zen approach is entirely keeping with American pragmatism.

That is haiku's essential koan. The thing itself, passing— neither a glorification nor denigration of the material world. No metaphors for the fallen world or the divine. The "Heart Sutra" says *form is emptiness and emptiness form.* Kerouac's meat wheel of samsara and nirvana are not separate but simultaneous. Or, to put it in Western terms, the sacred and profane are one. The western philosophical dialogue between human and nature presupposes separation of the two as tacit reality when really we constantly share and merge energies that manifest in myriad forms be they beautiful or horrific. Energy cannot be destroyed. It merely changes shape. Haiku is not what the poet says about nature as much as it is nature speaking through the poet. Therein Heisenberg's indeterminacy principle, *the observer cannot observe without altering the observation.* Haiku render the undifferentiated experience of observer and scene. The common *thusness.* The trick is to acknowledge the ego, forgive it for obtruding, laugh at its fears, pretensions, and willful artifice and involve it in the process. In that way, your true nature, your original face, can experience the essence you ultimately share with nature. Haiku finds that ultimate reality in the ordinary expression. No big deal. No mean feat.

Haiku

wet sand raven tracks
amid just fallen maple leaves,
deeper where it lifted

low gray skies over
miles of corn stubble, old woman
peering into mailbox

my shadow in waves
over limestone shore
does not wash away

bare birch mountainside,
breath hovering over snow,
words never spoken

kudzu has crossed
the Ohio, climbs the screen
of a closed drive-in

after its caw
the breath of a crow
hangs on winter air

memorizing your face
with kisses in the dark
the morning I leave

blowing out the candle,
dry rose petals fall, strumming
dulcimer strings

Driving the Midwest,
all thoughts flatten to one—
drive through it

Old Joe the stray dog
flops down bad hips on mattress
still warm from my bones

Kerouac, we knock
your pickled bones together,
Tibetan be-bop

Letter Left On the Porch of the Kerouac House

So as I sit still on the porch
in the faint breeze cooling
the outskirts of downtown
Orlando, gray moss swaying
from this 300 year old live oak
like American *bhikku* beards
that speak the long vowels
only stretched ears of Buddha
can hear, I ponder one word
to give at the end of this road.

One word as small as the seed
I once spit from this porch.
Smell those orange blossoms wafting
beneath the skyline of high-rise banks,
the tallest adorned with black horns
like Moloch, white church spires
below mirrored in its glass sides,
here on the whirl-pooling edge
of the Disney vortex—wheel
of samsara that spins all matter out.

I was broke when I came here
and never really made enough
dough for more than a good bender
though the estate sold the original

teletype manuscript of *On the Road*
to a football mogul for 2.6 million.
I never genuflected at the altar
of the almighty dollar when I prayed
down on my beat knees by the end.

But there is no end, only the golden
scripture unrolling and outlasting
the teletype, the live oak, and horned
cash cow. For what is the commerce
of eternity? Ask Walt Disney,
who plunked down his dream
of automated fun in the middle
of panther extincting swampland
that became an empire so rich
he could freeze-dry his remains
in a crypt under the magic kingdom.

What would Walt Whitman say,
who praises the live oak arms
upraised in steady ablutions,
as he hands out one carnation
with every Sunday newspaper
he sells at the intersection
of Colonial and I-4 as America
rushes by towards Autogeddon?

The same meat wheel spun them
both to this sense realm.
The black and white cat sitting
on the car top lives also no less,
nor the chameleon scuttling over
dry leaves stopping to tilt its head
and bat a translucent lidded eye
in a wink of awakening I saw
as the world refracted in a drop
of sweat dangling my eyebrow,

prism of light that flesh is heir to.
Open your eyes and close them—
there's being and nothingness
in a nutshell, but for that one drop
at heart, Avolokiteshvara's tear
that booze could not blot out.
That summer I would shower
six times a day, waiting for rain's
chant to cleanse the ignorant
steam of mind, listening for that,
blatting of motion and stillness.

What good the teletype roll recording
the road traveled, or even this letter,
a goodbye as soon as a howdy do,
our comings and goings condensed
to a postcard of live oak and shack—
Wish you were here? Guess what,
dharma bum, you are! And the word
that bubbles up from the bottom
of spring-fed Lake Adair, this clear
breath bursting empty sounds...*still*.

The Ordinary

Another Monday another mundane
parade we join knowing it ends
in the ordinary where lines
in the face of the stranger
in the mirror mark the miles
shuffled and so much undone.
But outside, over the fenced yard,
across the street, a child begins singing.

Caught between the wind billowing
curtains and dishes in the sink,

you stare hard at the crumbs of bread
on the board and pieces of sky seen
through bare branches and return
to that empty parking lot,
chasing a gull feather around just
to cup the ocean in your hands.

We both bit into that fruit of desire
despite the worm crying *forbidden.*
Now we cut it into sections
of his and hers, throwing away
the core, forgetting the bliss
of gazelle eyes glazing over
in the lion's jaws, those tears
of surrender blending with blood.

So we fall into alone and
separate begets pain, begets
avoidance of pain and we live
for happy hour, braking only
for sirens, not ours, not yet,
pulling over, rolling down the window
to glimpse a red rubber ball
in the middle of a landfill.

Some days the sky is merely
the lid over what we must do
for the things we think we need
until suddenly it spreads wide
and we are standing in that field
catching our breaths, giddy and
dizzy as we kick that red ball
we thought lost so long ago.

Skinny-Dipping the Ganges

Too many times I simply cannot think
without thinking. Biceps and thighs break
free of this as I dive and stroke
up through the cold spring, sun filled pond,
pale flame of body
burning underwater.

Then, there they are, sides glinting—
a dim arc curling, cluster
of sharp flashes scattering—
and I see how thoughts
come to light
then angle back
into green blending to black deeps
and again rise

where ice-melt sings flashes
clear down from the Himalayas
in the thrum of minnows
the current carries to the plain of the Ganges
where a young woman,
so used to the task,
balances a plaited reed basket
full of silver slivers
on her head
as she scuffs along the dust

thinking of nothing,
humming to herself
beside a river that always finds
the easy way—swallowing
villages, birthing fields—
while the sun fires
the whole time
as thought itself.

Tom Montag

Biographical Sketch

Tom Montag was born and raised on an Iowa farm, the eldest of nine children. "I grew up with Iowa dirt under my fingernails, Iowa wind in my hair, the well-chewed talk of Iowa farmers in my dreams. I can only be what I am, which is 'a minor regional poet.'"

In both his poetry and prose, Montag explores the interplay and resonance among place, voice, and meaning. His sensibility was marked early by the directness of experience in his farm childhood, by the rhythm of the those days and chores and seasons, and by "the longing that comes of watching a far horizon." *Curlew: Home* (Mid-day Moon Books, 2001) is the memoir of his first fourteen years. In *Middle Ground* (Midwestern Writers Publishing House, 1982) Montag sustained other voices in addition to his own—farmer, Civil War soldier, pioneer widow. *Between Zen and Midwestern* (saltworks, 1981) started teasing out the Zen/middle western connection that culminates in his newest collection, *The Big Book of Ben Zen* (MWPH Books, 2004). *The Sweet Bite of Morning* (Juniper Press, 2003) is a selection of "Plain Poems" from his daily examination of the same stretch of ground where he lives in Wisconsin over the course of a year. Montag's essays about writing and being a writer were published as *Kissing Poetry's Sister* (Joint Venture, 2002). He is also at work on *Vagabond in the Middle*, a five-year prose project to see what makes us middle western; progress is reported regularly at **http:// middlewesterner.blogspot.com**. Montag worked in printing for 25 years as a pressman, supervisor, manager of customer service, and training director before retiring in October, 2002, at age 55 to take up writing full-time. He lives in Fairwater, Wisconsin, with Mary his wife of more than thirty years. The couple has two grown daughters, Jenifer and Jessica.

Zen Statement:The Stroke I Make

I don't know enough to say I am a Zen Buddhist. I know enough to think the middle western farmer and the Buddhist monk would find much to talk of. Both monk and farmer understand that, as my Ben Zen says, "nothing matters and everything matters." Both have seen the wheel turn, everything going 'round the great circle. Both live close to the earth and grasp the essential simplicity of things; neither is confused by charade at the surface.

I come from a place bold with green crop and black soil, tawny autumn and grey distance, fiery sunset—bold with statement, but not much for explanation. A world where it rains or it doesn't.

Given the farmer's silence, it's a wonder the farm boy ever comes to speech at all, much less to poetry. "If you say anything, you've said too much," Ben says, remembering the tax assessor asked the farmer "Do you think it will rain?" and the farmer replied "It'll be a hell of a long dry spell if it don't."

Meditation and plowing corn stubble are not so different.

My understanding of Zen has given me not beliefs, but ways to embrace the world. Direct apprehension in a sudden moment. Calmness, serenity, strength. Detachment and engagement. A way to see and to respond to what I see. Not the content, but the form of it. Not the paint on the brush, the artist would say, but the stroke I make of it.

A Selection from the *Ben Zen* Poems

*

The monk's bowl
Is never empty,

Never full.
He's no fool,

Ben Zen says,
Follow him!
*

Sometimes the carpenter
Has only a hammer.

Sometimes the hammer
Is not enough.
*

Desire
Destroys a man

Twice: once
In the wanting,

Then again
In the not letting go.
*

O, to be the junkman, Ben says,
To have everything no one wants.
*

I push the mountain,
Ben says, and push

The mountain and
Still the mountain

Pushes back.

*
When you have enough
You have too much.

Leave a few
Grains of rice,

Leave the last
Sip of wine.
*
You are welcome,
The holy man said,
To all the wood I have.

I have no fish either.
*
The more I know
The more I know

I know nothing.
*
This is my curse,
Says Ben. I can

Believe things
I cannot understand,

I can understand things
I cannot believe.
*
That which is
Offered, being

Offered, is no
Longer the gift.

The gift was
The offering.

*

Do not worry of tomorrow—
It will end where it began,

In waiting for the light.

A Selection from "Plain Poems: A Fairwater Daybook"

*

APRIL 30, 2001 (1)

The hawk is present in its absence.
The hawk tree is here as emptiness.

Mindfulness, like a cup full of wind—
I've got the form of it this morning.
*

MAY 9, 2001 (4)

The trees! They crowd us, they pack the distance tight.
They change the sky, they change the meaning of light.
*

MAY 25, 2001 (1)

The sun this
morning is

less story
than silence.

A fellow
wants to

tell too much.
    *

JULY 6, 2001 (2)

We don't know the ponderous
thoughts of stones. What do they

dream of as afternoon heats them?
Do they dream of arms and legs

or wings? Do they dream of love?
Do they remember glaciers—

the weight, the shove? Sitting with
stones, oh, lost among stones, aren't

you surprised at what you learn?

Shin Yu Pai

Biographical Sketch

Shin Yu Pai born in 1975, is a 2nd generation Taiwanese-American poet and photographer. She grew up in Southern California and studied at The Naropa Institute, before receiving her MFA from the School of the Art Institute of Chicago.

Her first full-length collection of poetry, *Equivalence,* (La Alameda, 2003), explores the intersections between visual arts and language and Eastern and Western traditions. A chapbook of her translations from ancient Chinese poetry, *Ten Thousand Miles of Mountains and Rivers*, was published in 1998 by Third Ear Books. A special edition letter-pressed, hand-bound chapbook, *Works on Paper*, is forthcoming from Convivio Bookworks.

As a visual artist, her work has appeared in galleries throughout the Midwest including Gallery 2 and The Three Arts Club of Chicago. A portfolio of her photography can be viewed at **http://www.zonezero.com.** She has been awarded grants from the Cambridge Arts Council, the Union League Civic and Arts Foundation and the Puffin Foundation, in addition to residencies from The MacDowell Colony, The Ragdale Foundation, and the Provincetown Fine Arts Work Center.

Current projects include "Nutritional Feed," a visual text project with painter David Lukowski, "Unnecessary Roughness," a collaborative manuscript authored with New York photographer Ferenc Suto, and an opera with Chinese composer Gao Ping.

fall aster with firefly

A scroll passes hands in
Chionji, street market, Kyoto
faded paper mounted over
homespun coarse-dyed cotton
bands of brown and
green, earth and moss
a wet fox-hair brush
dipped in ink and
drawn across paper one
hundred years ago the image
fanning outwards a
firefly at rest on the
leaf of a pink aster bloom
swaying in wind
ichi go ichi e
one meeting
one opportunity—
the months in which
they courted a
season for fireflies
winged, nocturnal beetles
emitting a soft, bright light
brought home to hang
where incense burns
blow out the incense stick
this home lit by the heat
of fireflies

circle, triangle, square

when Sengai put brush to paper
he drew three forms, overlapping
square, triangle, circle

a koan for disciples
for scholars to argue and
decipher throughout the ages

the temple walls are four-
sided, within them sit
and practice

upon achieving a mind
of enlightenment, see
the circle, an empty teaching

the trinity,
and the confines of
earth-bound existence, *or*

circle
triangle
square

a lesson
in geometry
intended for children

Poem
                    for Wolfgang Laib

a life
of collecting pollen
from hazelnut bushes
a life of gathering word-grains
to find all you have wanted
all you have waited to say

five
mountains

we cannot climb
hills we cannot touch
perhaps we are only here
to say house, bridge, or gate
a passage
to somewhere else
yellow molecules
spooned and sifted
from a jar filled with

sunlight
pouring
milk
over
stone
you are the energy
that breaks form
building wax houses
pressed from combs

a wax room
set upon a mountain
an offering of rice
nowhere everywhere
the songs of Shams

Paul S. Piper

Biographical Sketch

"I was born in Chicago in 1951, but the city with all its charms and diversions was never a fit. In 1969, after graduating from high school, I moved out to Missoula, Montana, to attend the University of Montana. After a dismal encounter with Forestry as a major (imagine walking through a pristine ponderosa forest determining what each tree is worth as timber), I entered an experimental interdisciplinary program with an environmental and wilderness bent called The Round River Program. One of the visiting faculty, Gary Snyder, wasted no time setting up a 6:30 a.m. zazen group. Gary provided minimal instruction, as well as introducing us to some sutras and texts by D.T. Suzuki. The core of that group continued to sit for the next fifteen years or so as the Missoula Zen Group. That we were teacherless was viewed both as an obstacle and a blessing. Subsequent travels brought me in contact with Genki Roshi at the Seattle Zen Center and Roshi Robert Aitken at the Diamond Sangha in Honolulu. Various career shifts led me to Bellingham, Washington, where I am currently a librarian at Western Washington University. I also act as librarian for the Bellingham Dharma Center, an umbrella for four diverse Buddhist groups.

"I have written poetry ever since high school, and after studying briefly with Richard Hugo in the 70's, I finally obtained an MFA in 1992. Whether this destroyed my ability to write decent poetry remains to be seen."

Paul Piper's recent collection of poems is: *Now and Then* (Bellingham, WA: Flying Trout Press 2004).

Zen and Poetry Statement

Reflecting on Joseph Goldstein's exploration of American Buddhism in his recent book *One Dharma*, I think American Zen is in that same period of self-discovery, and as such any definition of it is by nature transitory. My own interest is with a Zen practice that is gradually divorcing itself from Asian cultural trappings.

I think Zen is a brilliant synthesis of wildness and discipline. To my mind, wildness becomes wilderness, and an American Zen is wilderness (ecologically & environmentally) oriented. But wilderness requires preservation, and that requires discipline. And the discipline of sitting over a number of years becomes a doorway into another wilderness–that of mind. There is a sacred place for nature within the world of Zen. Original nature. What we are.

In a book on the *paramitas* Sheng-yen mentions that we are made of the same stuff as nature, we are of nature, and that our connection to the nature is irrefutable. Yet westerners insist that they inhabit a unique and separate "self," a concept that is reinforced every minute of every day. American pop culture, with its materialistic, me-oriented, surface-oriented, fashion-oriented milieu will perhaps be the most challenging one for Zen to inhabit. But Zen also has the capability of transforming that very culture. I believe that it can and will.

While I don't believe that we can separate a "self" from original nature, I also don't believe I can any longer separate Zen from life. Zen is not just time spent on the cushion or reading Zen books. So there is difficulty determining just what a "Zen" poem is. For that reason, and for the sake of this anthology, I have included poems that derive fairly directly from the experience of zazen, or feature Zen specifically in the content.

there is no ripple on the world
for Bill Eleson

Last night Ryokan
gave me the moon
after I stole his shirt—
I have yet to thank him

Everyday we are given countless gifts
from the mindless *Tathagata*
we fail to acknowledge—
blind sheep, running into walls
staring into voids, seeing nothing

Bird call falls away, wind
drops off, body and
mind turn to dust,
dust blows away.
Where have they gone?

Amusing,
there is nothing
to hold us, echo us.
There is no ripple on the world.

Bowing

I bow to the wall I face, to the life I face

I bow to the vertical grain
  of wood, stretching from earth
  to sky

I bow to the hands of the artisan that sanded
  this wood, that stained this wood, hands

that held flesh, brushed away
   tears, kept out the night

I bow to the noise I enter, I bow
   to the silence that encompasses the noise.

I bow to the scraps of my life, little
   boats, that they may journey safely home.

I bow to each breath, the first breath,
   the last breath, the space between
   breathing where the other world lies.

I bow to my suffering, to my weakness
   in suffering, to the end of all suffering, for
   all the sentient beings.

I bow to nothing, no idol, no statue, no dharma,
   I bow to nothing, I do nothing
   but bow.

The Morning Star
   in honor of the Buddha's enlightenment

Not a star but a planet   not
a planet but an eye   not an eye
but a voice   not a voice but a resolute
silence

         aligned with the moon, an empty bowl
         of light

Not a star but a wish   not a wish but water
washing over us   not water but a promise   not
a promise but a stone falling through water

aligned with the mind the ripples
    are infinite

Is a bell. Its single note floats in water
falling through a stone. There are echoes
everywhere. A flower held aloft. Dust falling
through the mirror.

    aligned with the heart, a door that swings
    in, out,
    easy on its hinges. A door
    that isn't even there.

Christmas Eve, 2003

Green lights strung in an apple tree
    trace a swan opening
to flight

or hope. Blue lights above a garage, the depth
    of mind, also blue.
Red lights

frame the doorway of desire. They
    wink
as I walk away. White

lights everywhere, sparking
    the still air, all
the stars I've lost or never had. The sky

ever darkening is the emptiness
    I rise out of, fall
into, a thousand times a day.

Maj Ragain

Biographical Sketch

Photo by Jim Lange

"I was born on a Saturday morning, September 15, 1940, the son of Daniel Wayne Ragain, a carpenter, and Beatrice Lucille Totten Ragain, a homemaker, in Olney, a small farming community in southeastern Illinois. I was bitten by polio, 1948, grounded and home tutored till high school. The solitude led to living in my head, reading and making up worlds through which to roam freely. One summer, in my mid teens, I read Hitler's *Mein Kampf* and Gandhi's *Autobiography*, one after another. The life of the mind opened right there: a realm of deathless words; a sense of kinship far beyond our small family in its struggles for bread and coal; a notion that a man might shape his life through his choices, that we become our choices; that we get what we do, not what is promised; that trust and spirit are insolubly linked.

"More books, a gift of *The Rubaiyat of Omar Khayyam. There was the Door to which I found no Key; There was the Veil through which I might not see.* It was my first bite of the Sufi apple, that Golden Delicious. Then, in college, I stumbled onto Paul Rep's wonderment *Zen Flesh, Zen Bones*, then Kenneth Rexroth's *One Hundred Translations from The Chinese* (and another collection from the Japanese), poets who seemed to have written poems anticipating my reading them, that odd sense of direct transmission. I rode John Blofeld's shoulders across Taoist China, back into the mists. Lao Tzu found me through the pages of the *Tao Te Ching…Simplicity comes from letting go of what you want.* Before long I had wandered into the foothills of Cold Mountain in Chekiang province, a two day hike from the East China sea. Cold Mountain is in Han-Shan's poems. Cold Mountain is the poems. Cold Mountain is Han-Shan. All of this is in the mind. I am still in the foothills. If my heart were like Han-shan's, I'd be on that mountain right now. The highest art is to quicken, deepen the days we are given. I must not forget to heed Han-Shan's last words, shouted to the emperor's messengers, before he disappeared into a crevice of Cold Mountain. *Thieves. Thieves. You better get to work"*

Maj Ragain lives in Kent, Ohio, and teaches writing and poetry at Kent State University. His most recent book is *Twist the Axe: A Horseplayer's Story: Poems and Journal* (Bottom Dog Press 2002).

Zen Statement: Everyday Life Is the Path: Notes on Zen Buddhism and Poetry

Whatever small understanding I have of Zen Buddhism is embodied in my poems. The poems know; I don't. Like Yeats in his letter to his old friend Lady Pelham a few weeks before his death, my conviction is that a man's life may embody a truth, but that man cannot know that truth. The truth, the Tao, the dharma, are, thankfully, larger than any one life. There are many on the path, yet that journey into the interior is also solitary. This yoking of solitude and community is one of the gifts of Zen Buddhism. As Gary Snyder remarks, "We are all fellow workers in the Buddha fields." It is work without merit. It is the cultivation of an inner life, not in the cloistered garden of Christianity, but in a boundless field where the countless *sangha* bend to pluck the jeweled strawberries of compassion.

Some sing as we work. Writing poems, handling the fruit of words, is a cultivation of heart and spirit, of a ground at once communal and personal. The *sangha* is a fellowship, literally an aggregate, of those past, present and those to come who seek the way. We all sit together. We make poems together. Bodhidharma found his way into China by 479 AD. The paintings in the Dorgonne caves date back to 26,000 BC, notes Robert Bly, images, word pictures, animals, men, hunting, the mystery of living in the world. Two ancient unbroken traditions, one turning inward, seeking a mind as transparent as breath, the other directed outward, finding images, word pictures. The two strands intertwine ever more intricately through the practice of making the poem and the practice of meditation. My own poems are attempts to wishbone the traditions of Zen to American idiom. On the page, all things are contemporaneous. It is always high noon. The poems are struggles to wake up, emblems of awareness, tattered prayer flags in the bone white light of the moon that never wanes. The mind of the reader and that of the writer meet in the metaphor. The mind of the teacher and that of the student meet in the koan. Mumon's comment from Paul Rep's *Zen Flesh, Zen Bones* is this:

> When the question is common
> The answer is also common.
> When the question is sand in
> A bowl of boiled rice
> The answer is a stick in the soft mud.

Ordinary mind is the way. The lotus is rooted in mud. Tonight, a full April moon shines across the fertile emptiness. Outside my window, an iron tree blooms.

[April 3, 2004]

Don't Expect Anything

The first day of summer
we uproot the sweet annie herbs
in the plant barrels.
They have outgrown themselves into seed.
A tumble of yellow jacketed hornets
fills the air, the top of their mountain
blown into the heavens.
They fly like drunken fish, sperm,
blind lost pilots from the galaxy
that labors inside this one.

Spring is gone. Nothing works.
My lessons fumble along.
I am trying to learn to bow,
to give myself up.
I empty myself out the top of the head
and right myself, ready to be filled.
I must be prepared to bow,
even in my last moment,
to pour the old rancid coffee of self desire
onto the ground where I stand.

When I don't know what else to do,
I bow.

A String of Ordinary Words

When the Samurai walked into battle,

they carried small purses
containing money for their funerals.

The two virtues are *Katannu,*
knowing our debt of gratitude,

and *Kataredi,* trying to repay it.
These sustain the world.

In the beginning, take the teacher as teacher.
In the middle, take the scriptures as teacher.
In the end, take your own mind as teacher.

Soon, like a hair pulled out of butter,
leaving everything behind,
you'll go on again alone.

"If You Cannot Find the Truth Right Where You Are,
   Where Do You Expect to Find It?"
      —Dogen

Find it in the letter the mailman refused
to deliver. Go chase him down the sidewalk.
Take back what belongs to you.

Find it in the Goodwill, the dead man's suits
without shoulders, hung in a row.
Check the left breast pocket. Wear that one home.

Find it in the grocery, underneath the cart
where you stow the potatoes and the cat litter.
Sometimes the truth is low down.

Find it on your backstep, the one black shoe
heavy as a stone, the laces in a hard,
hard knot.

Find it in yesterday's half frozen cup
of muddy coffee you left on the porch rail.
Drink it down. Shoulder the morning.
A clear, blind river runs beneath your feet.

Find it in your own breath,
the windhorse that carries you
across this plain, toward the mountains.

If you cannot find the truth where you live,

where does it live, this truth you live for?

A Hungry Ghost Surrenders His Tackle Box

My friend Bill Hupp leaves this week,
a year's stay, Zen Mountain Monastery,
nestled in the Catskills.
He must surrender his things before
he can give himself away, cut his ties
to the world, gray house on Longcoy Street,
green Ford, bachelor's kit and kaboodle.
He must now trust the sangha,
the community with whom he will train
to live the four noble truths,
to dig through the compost heap
of his suffering and cart it away.

This rainy March afternoon
Bill lays down his burdens at my house.
I am to find solace in attachment
to what he must renounce.
A two foot stack of *Tricycle*,
the Buddhist review, thousands of bent
word keys to the Pure Land, how to shoe
the windhorse, how to jumpstart
the dharma in your neighborhood.

He hands me a sheaf of his own
pissed off, gotta bless you anyway poems,
fuel for his heart's fire.

He drags in a rolled up, inflatable
rubber raft, a ten footer, heavy duty,
Lake Erie tested, with red oars
and a handy foot pump: three hundred
should do it. Bill gives me his tackle box.
Fishing is an attachment which he must sever.
Otherwise, he'll remain a hungry ghost
hiding a can of worms, sneaking out of sesshin
to fish the monastery pond.
I accept his gift because I must,
a big, multiple drawer Plano stuffed
with plastic worms, crusty jars of pork rinds,
jointed minnows, silver bucktail spoons.
I open it once, then consign it in the basement.
Belongings, the little one word book of law.

We must be our longings.
I don't know another path.

Bill, don't forget to come back
for what you belong to,
rubber raft, tackle box, words,
the rest of this stuff
which, as the Buddhists teach,
are phenomena that rise and set
only in the mind.

David Ray

Biographical Sketch

"My childhood in Oklahoma and teen years in Arizona are described in my 2003 memoir, *The Endless Search* (Soft Skull Press) and in an autobiographical essay in *The Dictionary of Literary Biography* (Gale Research). I moved to Arizona for my health at fifteen, then attended the University of Chicago on a scholarship and undertook a career of teaching, editing, and writing. A University of Vienna and Woursell Foundation fellowship enabled me to live the expatriate life in England, Greece, and Spain in the late Sixties. I returned to teach at Iowa's Graduate Writer's Workshop and the University of Missouri-Kansas City, and in India, Australia, New Zealand.

"With Robert Bly I co-founded American Writers Against the Vietnam War in 1966 and participated in and encouraged anti-war readings and demonstrations. My books of poetry include *One Thousand Years: Poems About the Holocaust* (Timberline Press, 2004), *Demons In The Diner* (Ashland Poetry Press), *The Tramp's Cup* and *Wool Highways* (both winners of the William Carlos Williams Awards) and others. I was founding editor of *New Letters* magazine and have edited several anthologies, including *Fathers: A Collection of Poems* (St. Martin's Press), co-edited with Judy Ray.

"*Sardanapalus*, poems about the Iraq wars, is forthcoming from Howling Dog Press. *After Tagore*, transcreations, is forthcoming from Nirala Publications in India, and Pudding House Press has published my work in their *Greatest Hits* series. I live in Tucson with my wife, Judy, and often travel for workshops and readings."

Statement: Poetry and Zen

My interest in Zen has for decades been inseparable from my writing and search for serenity. Although Western philosophers and therapists give us a clue now and then as to how to accept our place in the universe, it is Zen that comes closest to offering the real secrets— the ones we don't notice because they're so obvious. Live in the moment! Whatever it is, let it go! My transcreations (it would be presumptuous to call them translations) from other languages try to capture a quality that Longinus called sublimity, but I call Zen. R. H. Blyth speaks well of this.

Temperamentally, I am ill-suited to learn from Zen, but for that reason need it all the more desperately. When I read those who stake a claim to some wisdom derived from Zen, though, I am suspicious. Get hold of something and it's human to take it to market, but that's Zen too. The guru speaks of detachment but seldom fails to mention his rather impressive possessions. I finally understood the meaning of "If you meet the Buddha on the road, kill him!" when I heard a self-styled guru giving his audience ALL the answers. Such presumption seemed very presumptuous and non-Zen to me.

All through my poems are lines that are like escape valves, just as in a woven rug there's an outlet for the spirit. The weight of our attachments lades a poem, but there's often a line of release. In the best of all possible worlds that one line would be sufficient for the reader, no need for the load of false reality, what Kierkegaard called "the lower domains of pettiness." In "Twigs," e.g., a poem which includes stealth bombers and friendship betrayed, the release line from such realities is: "But live in the now, the very much now!" If only we could!

I once received a review copy of Robert Bly's *Silence In The Snowy Fields,* and the book was all blank, nothing but whiteness like snow, a publisher's error, and yet perhaps that was the ideal poem, speaking with silence. An empty room is pure Zen, but we move into it and it is soon chaos and clutter. And that too is Zen, like a poem overwhelmed by the demands of formalist verse.

A Journey With Basho

Basho, please take me
along once more on that path—
Edo, here we come!

Yes, Sunflower Hill—
So it says—but I see none,
while you're still looking.

Clear your head of this—
It's a fool's notion that we
can't stop too often.

There's no time for that—
night under the moonstruck roof
where the red light glows.

Quit counting dim stars!
There's enough work for your eyes
right here on the path.

One chrysanthemum
is all I have, and she'll serve
no hot tea for that.

No free tea until
I said she must be joking—
"Surely not sixty!"

Stare at that new rice
all you want, but it will not
be ready in time.

Pausing by strange graves
we don't care if they're strangers.
We weep anyway.

Why does gratitude
occur to me only now—
too far and too late?

One night apart then
was unbearable. One month
now is sufficient.

One broken strap, Friend,
is no excuse for spending
on *two* new sandals.

Someday they will pay
poets, you say as the wind—
even the wind—laughs.

So many—places
where one would not mind dying,
yet we pass them by.

I left the sad one—
but you have the greater grief.
You left the dead one.

She said I left her,
but in truth I was the one
more to be pitied.

Speak nonsense elsewhere.
Counting petals never tells
how many years left.

Still counting those miles
proving you have learned nothing
since we two set out.

You can't paint a stroke—
some excuse—that these mountains
are beyond man's scope.

Among other sights,
a castle. But of what use?
Wind blows through turrets.

The recluse announced
he was forsaking the world.
Such words make crows laugh!

Such wealth on this trip!
One day buy mountains, next day
blue harbor with boats.

Sixth day of new moon.
What an odd time to take leave.
Make it the seventh.

Such nonsense!—to think
the moon has only one task—
to shine on your poem!

Wait! Sniff around, down
in that hay, they've been gone no
more than an hour.

What joy to drink rain,
knowing poisons will never
rise high as dark clouds.

It's morning, damn it,
I forgot to bless sandals.
Basho, please forgive!

Wild cranes in the sky —
let's watch them part, then follow
their fine example.

Sad clam torn from shell,
say which of us is the shell
and which the poor clam.

Basho's in hospice —
I saw him today — so frail —
with hoarfrost on brows.

Leafy tree, enough!
One more leaf would do me in.
Poets must rest their pens.

Share the stars with me
tonight, Oh dog who looks down
sniffing the cobbles.

Dear dog and whisky,
even together you can't
replace old Basho.

Bartender praises
his long new bar as I grieve
dead wood and Basho.

Seido Ray Ronci

Biographical Sketch

Seido Ray Ronci is the director of Hokoku-An Zen Center in Columbia, Missouri, and adjunct professor at the University of Missouri where he teaches mythology, literary studies, and Postmodern American Poetry. His poems have appeared in *Ploughshares, Iowa Review, Rattle, Prairie Schooner*, and elsewhere. He has received an *AWP Intro Award*, an *Academy of American Poets Award*, and the *John H. Vreeland Award for Literary Composition* from the University of Nebraska. His most recent book of poems is *The World of Difference* (Pressed Wafer Press 2001).

As for Zen, Ronci says: "I went to a Catholic high school; on the first day of religion class Brother James walked in and wrote 'Religion is shit' on the blackboard. Then he walked out. The next day when he came to class he told us, 'I want you to forget everything you ever learned about religion, okay?' and walked out again. During that year we studied world religions. When we covered the section on Buddhism, and Zen in particular, I realized that I had always been a Buddhist. Throughout high school and college I read books on Zen and thought I had a good understanding of Buddhism. In my early 20s when I was bumming around Paris I realized my life, such as it was, was a disaster. All that I thought I 'understood' about Buddhism was intellectual bullshit. I had never found a teacher, had never learned to meditate. I vowed that when I returned to the United States I would find a master and learn how to sit down and shut up. That following summer I went to a talk at the Boulder Zen Center by Joshu Sasaki Roshi. I was 24. He has been my teacher now for 26 years."

Statement on Zen and Poetry

I'm a poet and I'm a Zen monk. I've been asked, "Are you a Zen poet?" I'm a husband, a father and a taxpayer. Am I a Zen taxpayer?

Buddhism teaches that when you wash your bowl, you should wash your bowl. Only that. This is what it means to sit still. This is what it means to practice: to give oneself completely to the task at hand. A Zen poet, like a Zen archer, will have learned from his or her ancestors, will have learned the forms, the techniques, the stories. Buddhism teaches that everything is practice. A Zen poet, in this respect, is like any other poet, or any other craftsman or technician—follow the form of the craft—practice, practice, practice. For the poet, that means paying attention to words and silence, rhythm and melody, line and space, over and over again, no matter how many times you miss the mark. The Zen poet, like any other poet, is a practitioner.

The Zen poet follows the rules of language and disappears in choices just like any other poet. Form is emptiness.

The Zen poet follows the form of sitting still for long periods of time in order to manifest zero and make the practice of zero the practice of a lifetime. Like any other poet: form is form.

The Zen poet perceives life from the point of view of sitting still. Language is but another form to be practiced. Infinite are all Dharmas. Like any other poet: emptiness is form.

The Zen poet practices form in order to forget form. Like any other poet: emptiness is emptiness.

Frog

   pond

      splash!

Old Monks Drinking

May I be born without hands for 500 lifetimes, for a
thousand more lifetimes, if to be without hands means
to need nothing yet give myself always to what's needed.

Bassui Roshi didn't fool around: *One who hands a glass of wine*
to another encouraging him to drink it will be reborn
for 500 lifetimes without hands. How many hundreds more
to he who hands the glass to himself?

At *Kogaku-An* he built a shrine to *Basshushin:* Lord
of the eternal hangover. As a brother monk once said:
"Sure, I'm a monk, but I never said I was a good one!"

He filled my teacup with *Courvoisier* and we stepped
outside behind the cabin for a cigar. All day zazen since
3:00 AM—chanting, working, sitting, sanzen with Roshi.

Every moment, including this one, a koan. We didn't speak.
We stood, sipped brandy from one hand and drew tobacco
from the other. Stared, mainly, at the black sky bright with

stars, satellites, passenger planes leaving LAX. So many
nights over 20 years standing in that spot—coyotes, scorpions,
pack dogs, bears, rattlesnakes, the outhouse breeze—pondering

the final destination of those planes. *Where is your home?*
The bell rings: More zazen! Standing on the mountain looking
into the jeweled valley with the burn of cognac and the bite

of tobacco on the tongue, blowing smoke. Two old monks.
In silence we finished; in silence we went to our bunks
and once again put the skeleton down.

Cricket

In the bush outside my window
you say the same thing over and over
with equal enthusiasm. Whatever it is,
I know it's the truth. No one could go on
so relentlessly if it wasn't.
What that truth is doesn't matter, finally,
because of your persistence.
I could hear you saying *"cricket-cricket"*
and translate it to, *"I am—I am!"*
And just as easily I could hear the chirping:
"Fuck it—fuck it!" and be equally moved
because I'm here by the window
where the stars are, where the half moon is.
Each morning, turning off the alarm,
stepping from the shower, drying myself,
tying my shoes, packing my bag....
When a car comes you become silent.
Too much noise shuts us both up.
Like you, I disappear all day.

Diamond Cutter

> *Listen: a nightingale strains her voice, serenading the snow.*
> *Look: a tortoise wearing a sword climbs the lampstand.*
> *– Hakuin*

The doctor came to take his pulse and said
"Everything seems fine." Winter, 1768.

In 3 days I'll be dead. Some doctor you are!

Ice on the branches, limbs bowed low,
the bald moonlight; the snowy wind,
the clatter and squeak of bamboo.

He woke and gave a shout
then turned on his side and died,
December 11th. Hakuin Ekaku.

> *If you want the great tranquility,*
> *prepare*
> *to sweat white beads.*

His last words—ashes the color of coral,
the scent of jasmine; just before going
he took up the brush and wrote:

> *Sitting still in the midst of this flaming world*
> *is a billion times better than sitting still in quiet.*

One *kanji—In the midst!*

By noon the ice had melted,
the branches stood tall again.

Becoming a Buddha

Suddenly one morning I woke up and I had ass-belly!
    That's when a man's ass decides it's had enough, leaves
his bottom, moves to his front and settles on his belly.
    After 40 or so years of reasonable comfort, the tired ass
leaves it up to the bones: "You do it, let him sit on *you*
    for a change." And the poor bones don't have a choice.
"Okay, ass," they say, "Be like that. You think *you've*
    had it bad! We're the last to go; we're the last to know
        the bastard's gone."

I sit here with arms folded over my newly relocated ass,
    and I finally understand the Buddha's big belly:
it takes this long to slow down and sit in the middle
    of the highway in rush hour, where traffic is a pin-drop

of sound, a solid brick of motion and there's no need,
      no desire to step on the gas and weave on through.
It takes this long to be reminded that soon enough
      it will be time to return this rented body to the dealer.

Now I have the Buddha's drooping ears to look forward to:
      old man ears, sacred elephant ears. Already my ears
are filling with hair. This is the forest where the Buddha sat.

      It happens, with enough time and in the right season,
that hearing hears itself.
      Then the earlobes become huge.

Andrew Schelling

Biographical Sketch

Photo by Laurita Fotografia

Andrew Schelling is the author of ten books of poetry, translation, and essay. He is an avid mountain explorer, student of natural history, ecology activist, translator of poetry from Sanskrit and related vernaculars of old India. Raised in Thoreau territory, west of Boston, his early influences were New England's resurgent conifer forests and the city's Asian art collections. From 1973 until 1990 he lived in Northern California, active with innovative poets in the Bay Area, much influenced by Language Poetry. Formal Zen sitting started in Santa Cruz with Kobun Chino Roshi, followed by regular practice at Berkeley Zen Center with Mel Weitsman. During the nineteen-eighties he and Benjamin Friedlander edited *Jimmy & Lucy's House of "K,"* an influential *samizdat* poetics journal. "We camped and hiked in the Coast Range and Sierra Nevada, and in 1986 did *padayatra* (trek-pilgrimage) in the Nepalese Himalaya. I make visits to India in search of poetry and lore with tracks back into the Paleolithic."

In 1990 he joined the faculty at Naropa University's Jack Kerouac School in Boulder where he teaches bioregional & journal writing, literature, and Sanskrit. His translations of classical Sanskrit poetry have won awards. "I sit zazen when possible at Hokubai Temple's buddha-yurt, watch for fox tracks, and live in the Front Range 'rainshadow' of Boulder, studying and writing at the feet of the Indian Peaks." Recent titles: *Songs of the Sons and Daughters of Buddha* co-translated with Anne Waldman (Shambhala Books 1996), *Tea Shack Interior: New and Selected Poetry* (Talisman Press 2002), and *Wild Form, Savage Grammar: Poetry, Ecology, Asia* (La Alameda Press 2003).

Statement on Writing & America Zen

I'd describe my poetry as setting up camp at the confluence of two traditions. One is North American projective writing from Thoreau forward. This would include natural history writings, the journals of explorers like Alvar Nuñez Cabeza de Vaca who learnt the continent by foot, and the innovations of the twentieth century poets. The other tradition is Asian, developed by mavericks of India, China, and Japan, who knew their Buddhism, visited the monasteries of their day, but held writing as their central practice. While training in poetry, I have sat with American Zen teachers Kobun Otokawa Roshi, Mel Weitsman, Philip Whalen, and Bernard Glassman. These days I get challenging instruction mostly from mountain spirits—sandstone, granite, gneiss, schist—who bring worthy teaching about stamina, changeable weather, vulnerability, and impermanence, to the Southern Rockies.

In the Rocky Mountains the least developed land lies at, should I say lifts into, high altitude. Designated Wilderness, Forest Service, or BLM—much of it is public property. The U.S. government holds it in trust for all of us. As a last refuge of true Constitutional equality, I take these serrated ridges & jutting peaks, sculpted cols & cirques, glaciers & alpine lakes, as our common holdings. We citizens wrangle over animal life, mineral resources, water rights, and timber. Here's one place I find poems waiting—they arise largely in journals—kept on excursions—into the heights or around the cities—alone, or with lover & friends.

How to convey *the wild game flavor* of this terrain? Its life forms adapted to low oxygen, scant moisture, intense sunlight, extreme ice? Scouring wind & a comforting thermos of tea? What about human themes, love, grief, humor, personal insight? The wider planet & its battered eco-zones? I believe it's what Thoreau found out a century & a half ago: for some of us *writing* is the way we learn our world, all trace of the fleeting, bluesy, present moment kept to the surface. Even if this means fragments, made up words, nonsense syllables, words lifted from far-off tongues.

Sarva mangalam: good luck to all beings.

High Up the Thunder Gods, Downstairs the Hunger

Dictionary is oracle bone. No entry falls between devout
and devour. And the three friends? Green enamel teapot,
buckskin gloves, sleeping bag of three decades. Not much
has changed. The human heart clings to its trouble, pitch
pine clings to the teapot. Back home I brush up on San-
skrit, look into Nagarjuna, & try to make sense. I can't
quite get it—is he saying the gods crave recognition?
From humans? Thunder growls off Indian Peaks; hail-
stones come hissing out of the heights.
And our scrap of darkness, what of it?

Hips, hiddenness, yours taken, mine given—
rain by the bed
lightning through

thrown open casements

Haibun the migration of haibun

Haibun is the Japanese literary form that mixes terse prose with
compressed verse. *Bun* stands for prose, *hai* is for haiku. I cannot
explain why the embedded verse does not simply ornament the
narrative. Nor, dear Kyle, can I answer why peaks in Colorado
swarm with bugs. Bugs? Flies anyhow. Curiously striped ocher &
black this one hangs in a blur of wings above a lichen patch. One
unforeseen route haibun took is Bear Peak via Fern Canyon.
Relentless. This happened fifty years after haiku went into
Japanese internment camps in Utah. Below, on Federal Land sits
the National Center for Atmospheric Research, a post-mod
edifice that bristles with satellite dishes. Haibun arrived here the
day the Dalai Lama visited. You could squint through stormy air

to the lichensize patch of lawn with its white tent. Thunder
cracked through Fern Canyon pinnacles that day. A falcon in the
aether. What did the Dalai Lama say?

> You must strive to live
> up to the name of the great
> Pandit Naropa—

*

Seventeen syllables.

Do the planet's precise messages all come encrypted in seventeen
syllables? If Donald Rumsfeld had time, he told the *Times*, he'd
sit down and figure out what he meant by the phrase, since it was
vital for the war with Iraq. Sort of like salmon fishing techniques,
haibun arrived along the Pacific Rim. Then drifted inland. Rogue
translators and barrels of oil got to the Front Range about the
same time. Today ranks of cumulous clouds hang stationary over
Indian Peaks. The prose is not there to explain the verse. The
Secretary of Defense is not there to explain the prose.

> "For the great motif of integrating many tongues into
> one true language is at work."

Haibun Flycatcher

How interesting that in 12th century Japan Saigyo remark'd,
"I know nothing about *depths* in the composition of poetry."
So dewdrop reflection of moon & wasted cherry blossom
quavering branch are the trace of a buddha passing through
our world?

What about piñon & various flycatcher species?

Today it is cottonwood boughs that seem wasted, withered
in the great mandala of drought. At the studio door a fly-

catcher leaps. Has he stopped over briefly, on his seasonal trip? Dear Marlow, songbirds migrate at night, while we are dreaming. How precious to meet you this lifetime. You & this eco-deity. The odds are improbable. The field guide says flycatchers are tough to distinguish. Encounter a nest, listen in on a love song, or let it go south with no name.

> Migration pilgrim road—
> what sort of creature
> gets to the end of it?

A temple administrator spoke through the dream. *Though all things in this world undergo change, the way of poetry extends unaltered to the very last age.* The Willow flycatcher's poem sounds like a "sneezy *fitz-bew*," but I'm starting to think it a *Cordillera*: that "thin, squeaky *pseet-trip-seet*." For sure it's a comrade to fly with.

> Bright eye-ring glint
> pale wing bar glance
> juniper pure land quiver.

27:xi:02

Huerfano Valley Seed Songs

> *for Joan Anderson & Robert Spellman*

1.

Curling barbed wire
cowboy bone
my lover's paintbrush I thought it.
Beginner's mind ash kettle,
something
goes past like the ghost of old love—
> one juniper seed I bring you

2.

Songs full of tiny
intricate thievery—
how else set sights on immortal?
bluestem grass Euripides
Sangre de Christos rubble of Aeschylus
Come back Norman O. Brown & teach us
a vocabulary to match high
arid mountains &
hungry ants—
cinder cone distances
        wavering heat

3.

These wrinkling mountains stretch north
carved up by glaciers,
aeons of good potable water
Who cares some traveler down here
left a yellow license plate
in the piñon dust?

Human sadness this year
        this year the cactus in bloom

4.

Once Mexico,
once Spanish land grant
& complicated water rights—
a pegmatite valley of old green ranches.
On the road kid
in black braids flagged us down.
Talk of butterflies—
Maitreya sits among cottonwood roots
oak leaves rattling by the

little spring.
Dear Frances Densmore
your Ute Indian bear dance book,
us walking the shade of Greenhorn Mountain
hulks of orange
earth-digging machines
   measure the decades.

5.

Seed songs
seed syllables
there will be many obstacles to this study of wisdom
in a good year the piñon nuts
will cascade into the pickup's bed
one cloud over Mt. Blanca
   promising rain

———————————————————————

OM   AH   HUM

Commentary

Past its southeasterly mouth many times, yes, but I hadn't drifted into the Huerfano until June. Entering to visit friends & camp on part of the former Santana Ranch, I began to watch for broken bits of verse—anything scattered about—like Frances Densmore had collected from Ute, Apache, Arapahoe, and pueblo people, all who had been into the region. (A sun dance still happens up valley.) It is a piñon-juniper zone, Gambel oak along the drainages, some aspen, lots of prairie cactus in bloom.

Huerfano, also name of the river that drains through, is Spanish—"orphan"—and refers to a singular, weird cinder cone that stands alone in the valley's flat southwards sweep. This was Mexico until 1848, the old-time ranch families still raising cattle after 400 years.

To the west the formidable Sangre de Christos; east the Wet Mountains; south the two snowcap Spanish Peaks. A *feng shui* consultant recently noted a significant line of influence between Blanca Peak, west, & in the east Greenhorn Mountain, near which in 1779 the New Mexico governor Juan Bautista de Anza killed the Comanche Cuerno Verde (Green Horn) for his notable headdress. "I recognized from his insignia and devices the famous chief Cuerno Verde, who, his spirit proud and superior to all his followers, left them and came ahead his horse curvetting spiritedly... I determined to have his life and his pride and arrogance precipitated him to this end."

Today the Buddhist retreat center Dorje Khung Dzong lies tucked into the faults, folds, fissures, & cones of Greenhorn.

Below Fourth of July Mine

Clark's nutcracker hid a seed
        400 years ago—
    twisty thick-trunk limber pine;

lightning sizzles along the broken granite ridge

cold hailstone hands;
    safe from storm tea;
that long gone bird who
    gave me shelter.

16:viii:03

Paul Skyrm

Biographical Sketch

"Re-entered Gaia, April 16ᵗʰ 1976, Mantua, Ohio, along the Cuyahoga River. Son to David James Skyrm Jr and Sandra Jean Giampapa Skyrm, brother to Raun David Skyrm & Marjorie Schotts Skyrm, grandson to Santo Anthony Giampapa & Rose Norma Giampapa, grandson to David James Skyrm Sr. and Mary Skyrm. Grew up in sandlot-gravel estate with maple tree size of Jack's Giant in front yard. Attended Kent State University and Jack Kerouac School of Disembodied Poetics at Naropa University Boulder, Colorado, majoring in English, left school for satori.

"Pilgrimages & meditations, solitary & with fellow narrow-path nomads, from Cape Cod knuckle fist to Mohave Desert old mind conversations with new mind and all the subtle-body Turtle Island transformations of mud & sky in the between.

Work in department store stock-house, warehouse, restaurant busboy dishwasher, as roofer, as headhunter in family business present home Aurora Ohio amongst a grove of family, friends, pretty women, tuliptree, maple, ironwood, heartwood, deer, raccoon, fox & bird."

Paul Skyrm has six manuscripts of poems and poetics including: *Dawn, Western Allegheny Plateau Book of Changes, Lilac Bushes in the Agony of Climb, Mind Poet Songs Owanka Wakan, Ukiyo-E* "all published in the Lotus Land, awaiting publication here on Earth."

Statement: Common Mind: The Good Work

Zazen in moon, three AM, fold legs as one. Upright. Bare-
bodied. Chant *OM MANE PADME HUM*—black clouds creep out
across nights illumination, zazen in void.

Turned down straight sheets, blue thread, four pillows folded
up and return pillows to morning, walk to bathroom, leave light off,
open curtains, white toothpaste drawn across white teeth, spit in sink,
water, fluoride, white wash beard face with white soap, spit, swab
ears, glasses wiped with vinegar and paper towel–the opening of clean-
liness, waste thrown with it's kind. Lift American Standard lid, stand
& ponder Buddhist idea of not engaging in whiskey—talk or sharing
lips with woman; sit & ponder, did I leave the whiskey on the bar
yesternight? Did I leave the girl on her porch step as well? Do I still
carry them with me? Breakfast of vitamins, juice, continue conversa-
tions with mom through house and yard, continue conversations with
dad through house and car. The significance of Zen in my poetics, put
pen down in silent reply. Zen in my poetics, return with pen & con-
tinue.

With work, at desk, phone rings, un-employed husbands &
wives, children mulberry bush and scream echo jostle frantic out-of-
workers to child mind, three PM. Climb up stairs, coffee with mom,
with dad spread seed for the finches, cardinals, blue-jays, thrushes,
grackles, sparrows, mourning doves, pileated woodpecker, chipmunk
& squirrel, corn for buck, doe & fawn. Wash hands, check messages
in disembodied ghost-voice box—messages from Brother Raun,
Steven, Maj, Bryan, Troy and Sarah quick breath hang-up. Gather for
supper on bamboo trays, blessings before consumption, oblations to
*BUDDANAM SARANAM GACCHAMI, DHARMAM SARANAM
GACCHAMI, SANGHAM SARANAM GACCHAMI, to the people
who made this meal creative, to the sharing of other forms of life
do I celebrate and eat and joy in supper talk.* Return calls, write
letters under tulip tree, bow to Sun and Moon in same sky, bow to
Gaia, trudge up stairs, good dreams to mom and dad, friends and
departed ones, inhale, exhale, sad breath glory.

Cross into meditation. Zazen in old moon.

Om Ah Hum Vajra Guru Padma Siddhi Hum

Terrors of the In-Between

Ambling within beech tree bouquet,
    shrouded nomads towering into oblivion harmonizing bagpipe
    kaddish behind mama & papa cathedral hilltop liberation smoke
    house gleaming,
I stare up finding shade & shadow break through heliotropic branches
    and fall into shoka ikebana leaving space for the dead to drink,
    the living to starve at supper table.

Amongst crazy wise brush broken shells
stale coyote shit hardened to gallstone twigs berries
    I find fox mortise-and-tenon skull free of flesh void of coarse
    nectarine coat
    overturned by stump silver prayer bowl over-flowing kernels

O! wont you nibble buck?
O! wont you suckle doe?

Howling wolf moon red-eyed marauder salivating burnt blood rears
in Western sky

skull in hands, flesh holding bone, Buddha free fall through vacant
parking lot saturated with rain fog settling out upon no-thing.

Hollowness where fox eyes saw good dreams, buck toothed hares
scurrying in the between life & death razor canines & loose meat
tongue

All around shrieks & howls empty bellies scouring dimly lit
world for wounded gazelles
broken bison summer sun cardinal flying too low above ground

All around hunters prowling four-legged hunters scavenging wings
spread mountain range circling overhead
All around weeping & slobbering wails my mother knelt at hunter
green marble two-body stepback urn gold nameplates translating
void

Santo Anthony Giampapa
Carey Grant paisanorth Boston hipster son of Sicily immigrant cousins
Alfonso & Rosalie locked in youthful embrace
O! where blue overalls worn white smell of old hot Monza motor oil
white curdled butcher coat stained with blood of lamb!

Rose Norma Caporale Giampapa
She who passed by her window morning yawn
all downtown boys squawking that Jane Russell took residence in
Michael & Jenny's Tapley Square south side parlor
O! where blackened lungs are broken angel wings breath is the explo-
ration & you need not wheeze in second story window peeing into
plastic bag chaffed by tube!

The Prayer for Refuge is a Tibetan prayer from the dead said for those
who continue Pilgrimage concealed behind bone & flesh thought &
jealousy hate & love
                    delusion & confusion.

the dead ask simply;
Now that I wander alone apart from my loved ones
And all my visions are but empty images
May the Buddhas exert the force of their compassion
And stop the fear and hate-drawn terrors of the between!

All around prayers of the disembodied ones
    whistle through trees Cap Anson tobacco card clothes-pinned
    onto bike spooks   hillbilly babies skipping over humpbacks in
    the Mediterranean

Tonight these beeches are Dracula's widows
    hunched & luminescent shriveled pasty
    grunting under moon & love, snarling for the un-dead prince
    who leaves not prayers but puncture wounds summoning infection.

Mother at the urn rise & leave these ashes swaddled in sheep wool
    here in the forest

May the demons heed their extremities devour the marble grenade!
May the demons throat be narrow so not even kusa grass blade may
pass!
May the demons wrench whirl cracked windpipe suffocation illumined
wolf moon!

May Spirit Fox never wander alone

May the demons awake & break into firefly

May all brothers sisters cousins aunts uncles pioneers shaman
tribesman
Firmly hold
Clasp hands round hulking backs sweet perfumed napes
gently rocking between

May Grandma Rose & Grandpa Santo never go hungry.
Tonight the dead pray for us.
> *[Aurora, Ohio,*Februrary 5, 2002 302
> Dwapara Yuga *4:57AM]*

Book II: White Rose

anarchy of the spirit no man is ascribed to be self-satisfying.

hours of jerking off & I still dream of high tides, brown-trout,
upstream's suffrage knowing she can never live as her daughter
and both are little rivers of the Silent Witness, deeper still,
Sarah's voices of communistic saints scanning the backbone of
nausea on Everglade
telling me my voice is what keeps her frightened of sleep.

patronica of the gutter, harmonisillica of second death's camp
zombies, word over the radio….Catholic Church sifting through
secret other-world wire tappings for second miracle to canonize
Mother Theresa……no one goes down in cardinal plumage to the

slum-miracle, Milagro peligroso, a dangerous benediction—the world
wrapped inside this world is the Oracle of the Wound, if you can hear me
Saint Francis black-toed & crucifixed of heart, La Verna is a silver nail in
the throat of Buddha!
a splinter of Christ femur stirring Original Poision in terminal ward
of Brahma where o where has our lamb conspired to drown new-
borns in the Ganges?

my White Rose, Maj Ragain, St. Francis growled in the birdbath this
morning for you!
redressing in his death-pelt, the beast-tunic which turned Francis into
Bear into Silence into Void he met me with where it was he could
find you & I lent to him some prospects.............listen for Howlin'
Wolf I told him, follow the spotted owl prints, look for burned down
houses & the Embarrass River, catch the Cuyahoga River on it's run
to East Grant Street a boulevard of loose rocks & ascension fern
crawling up elms & oaks where the White Rose may be twisted
bellied before fireplace & zoo writing prophecies to ministers &
Bodhisattvas, find out where the skeleton children fly-fish for Great
White Death for all I know it's this dharma-entanglement underneath
Vernor Lake of swamp & alligator & men who walk on their knees,
follow ole Melton's shit-talk & Shorty Nettleton's duck walk; watch
for Daniel Wayne Ragains he'll be leavin' the same way you're goin',
no mind barley & hops on his breath
see, there's a forgiveness for being alive for being able to experience
this human-life and this human-death
there's a confusion we all greet with & I found that confusion staring
into the window
after Francis took his hoof & beads on his way,
staring into my body through rusted stars & weathervanes I watched
my prick crawl out
from a cave of thornbush & maidenhair fern
stick out it's tongue tasting January snow & freeze
happy to be a prick.

I saw Death disarm this morning in the tabla of sky, behind a whirli-
gig clover of geese coming out of Lake Erie gown.

my White Rose, I took Buddha for a wife & Christ for a mistress
Allah perfumed thighs in the hall, Brahma panting toe-nails in the
sweat house
still I pant for that sweet morning glory bosom of Death
to kiss her pursed belly button
to wash her leather feet.

[Aurora, Ohio, January 7, 2004]

Larry Smith

Biographical Sketch

Photo by Ann Smith

Larry Smith grew up in the industrial Ohio Valley in the small town of Mingo Junction, Ohio, where he met and married his wife Ann. He worked two summers in the steel mills there, then went on to teach high school English in Euclid, Ohio. "I studied at Kent State University in the late 1960s, where I first heard Zen poet Gary Snyder read and talk, and was bitten by the Zen bug. I was at Kent in 1970 and was affected deeply by the demonstrations and shootings, and went on to complete a dissertation on Kenneth Patchen. Most of my work has been with alternative and engaged writing, including literary biographies of Kenneth Patchen and Lawrence Ferlinghetti. I've also been influenced by the life and work of Kenneth Rexroth as a man of letters and an activist writer." In 1985 Smith founded Bottom Dog Press, as an independent publisher, and has directed 90 books through the presses in their Midwest, Working Lives, and Harmony Series. He is a frequent reviewer of Zen publications in *Parabola* and *Shambhala Sun* magazines. In 2002 Smith retired from teaching literature and writing at Bowling Green State University's Firelands College, in Huron, Ohio, where he and his wife raised their three children.

"I suppose my Zen awareness grew through the writings of poets and translators, but also enlightened through some study at Zen Mountain Monastery with Daido John Loori and with the local CloudWater Zendo in Cleveland. Though books can't give it to you, they can help you find it in yourself. Teachers who write serve many of us lay Buddhists: Shunryu Suzuki, Taizan Maezumi, Charlotte Joko Beck, Pema Chodron, Sharon Salzberg, and so many others. I've kept my own practice going through meditation and writing poetry, and through a simple and direct listening to everyday life."

Smith's translations done with Taiwanese artist Mei Hui Huang, include *Chinese Zen Poems: What Hold Has This Mountian* (Bottom Dog Press 1998) and *Songs of the Woodcutter: Zen Poems of Wang Wei and Taigu Ryokan* (audio book with flute accompaniment by Monte Page; Bottom Dog Press 2003). His poems appeared in the previous American Zen anthology *Beneath a Single Moon* (Shambhala 1991). Smith's *Milldust and Roses: Memoirs* appeared in 2002 from Ridgeway Press, Detroit.

Zen Statement: Poems as Rocks

Twice recently I've been asked, "So in a nutshell—what is Zen?" I'm sorry, but I can't help laughing. Like the blues, if you have to be told, you won't get it. You may have to have that warm cup of tea thrown in your face or the door shut on you or sit with a koan for months or just learn to attend to your breathing in order to awaken. You'll find the path within, then without. I do believe my working-class family knew Zen without knowing it—my father working with tools, my grandmother's gentle caring, my mother's turning away tragedy with laughter. That's what I stay open to, the Zen of our true nature, what lies around us that is simple and true.

When my poems come into that centered and relaxed intention, they find their own path. Gary Snyder's "Riprap" poem says it—words like stones stacked along the trail to mark the way. The trick is to get out of the way, to remove the self-centered ego and join the larger Oneness. I go to the life we all share as my source. Zen has helped me get there, again and again.

> "Lay down these words
> Before your mind like rocks.
>   placed solid, by hands
> In choice of place, set
> Before the body of the mind
>   in space and time..."
>
> -Gary Snyder, from "Riprap"

In Muddy Waters

Was that a leaf or a bird
I ran over?

The radio cackles of an accident near home—
Could it be my son?

I watch the weather map
for my family and myself.

I mute myself through scenes
of people in Iraq, Liberia, Afghanistan...

A woman in the grocery store
slaps her son for talking loud.

My breath rises in my chest;
my shoulders tighten down.

I pull off the road
and feel the world's pain.

Like these lotus flowers
I must stand in muddy waters

bend with the winds or
harden till I break.

The bird inside my heart
still calls my name.

(8/22/2003)

Following the Road

I have left my wife at the airport,
flying out to help our daughter
whose baby will not eat.
And I am driving on to Kent
to hear some poets read tonight.

I don't know what to do with myself
when she leaves me like this.
An old friend has decided to
end our friendship. Another
is breaking it off with his wife.

I don't know what to say
to any of this—*Life's hard.*
And I say it aloud to myself,
Living is hard, and drive further
into the darkness, my headlights
going so far.

I sense my own tense breath, this fear
we call 'stress,' making it something else,
hiding from all that is real.

As I glide past Twin Lakes,
flat bodies of water under stars,
I hold the wheel gently, slowing my
body to the road, and know again that
this is just living, not a trauma
nor dying, but a lingering pain
reminding us that we are alive.

Calligraphy of Birds

Hundreds of starlings
stream across the sky,

their bodies turning colors
in the setting sun.

And I stand on the street
reading their flight
as my dog pulls his leash.

Their chatter among trees,
then small bodies rising
to sweep the sky and vanish.
What holds me so
while neighbors rake yards
and cars honk their horns?

In my sixth decade
my own path erases—
leaves swept by wind
into the lake.
Twin comfort of something larger
and not leaving a trace.

(3/6/2004)

Walking a Field into Evening

For learned books, I read the grasses.
For reputation, a bird calls my name.
I cross a stone bridge with the pace of dusk.
At the meadow gate, six cows meditate.

For decades I ran with my mind up hill and down;
now idleness lets me see what is near.
An arrow of wild geese crosses the sky,
my body still, my feet firm on the ground.

We age like trees now, watch our seedlings
take wind or grow around us.
I'm going to mark my books lightly

with a pencil. When someone wants
to take my picture, I'll walk towards them
and embrace. No more arguments
just heart sense, or talk about nothing.
Take walks in the woods at dawn and dusk,
breathe in the damp musty air,
learn to listen before I die.

(6/19/2003)

Into Still Air

The sounds
of magnolia blossoms
falling.

Yard birds
gather to feed
again.

A cardinal sings
in the moist air
before wind.

A dog barks
and then,
again.

The lawnmower
in a neighbor's yard
rests.

Dusk drifts in
like smoke
through trees.

Words
can't touch
it.

Tony Trigilio

Short Biographical Sketch

Photo by Elizabeth Lent

Tony Trigilio was born and raised in Pennsylvania. A child of a working-class immigrant family, he has studied Buddhism for 20 years, and practiced it for the past 10 years. He is a student of Geshe Tsultrim Chöephel, of the Kurukulla Center for Tibetan Buddhist Studies, in Boston. He has taught at Northeastern University, Kent State University, Bennington College, and, currently, at Columbia College Chicago, where he teaches poetry and literature, and serves as Director of the Undergraduate Poetry Program.

His poems have been published in journals such as *The Spoon River Poetry Review* (Illinois Feature Poet in the Spring '04 issue), *Rhino, Jack* magazine, *The Iowa Review*, and *The Beloit Poetry Journal*. His work also appears in the anthology, *A Gathering of Poets*, a volume commemorating the shootings at Kent State and Jackson State. He co-edits the poetry magazine *Court Green*, published in association with Columbia College Chicago, and has served on the editorial boards for the Samuel French Morse Poetry Prize and *Djinni* magazine. He is the author of a critical book on poetry and prophecy, *"Strange Prophecies Anew": Rereading Apocalypse in Blake, H.D., and Ginsberg* (Fairleigh Dickinson University Press), and reviews and articles in journals such as *American Literature, Modern Language Studies*, and *Tulsa Studies in Women's Literature*. He is co-editing an anthology of immigration literature, *Visions and Divisions: American Immigration Literature, 1870-1924*. A musician as well as a writer, he toured the U.S. several years ago with the band Drumming On Glass.

Statement: American Buddhism and My Writing

Among the earliest—and most anxious—moments in my Buddhist study and practice occurred when I read The Bodhisattva's Jewel Garland by the 11th-century Indian scholar Atisha, who says: "When among many, watch your words, / When remaining alone, watch your mind." The language seemed to encourage an exhausting level of self-surveillance. Yet as my practice became more disciplined, these words invited a rewarding ethos of mindfulness. My reaction to Atisha's words offers one way of describing myself as a U.S. Buddhist: sitting daily, I am taking part in a religious tradition that comes to me from cultures steeped in hierarchy, yet as an American and an artist, I find myself distrustful of hierarchies. I was drawn to Buddhism precisely because its governing notion of shunyata (emptiness) subverted the seemingly "natural" authority of hierarchies, especially those hierarchies that deluded me with the illusion that my identity was somehow separated from, and superior to, all other worldly phenomena. Guided by the notion that my "self" is empty of an essential existence, but with the "self" poised as a necessary force in the world, I work as an American Buddhist writer who sees the open field of the page as a space that fuses self-control and self-diffusion. I sit: I am solid and dissolute. I study Dharma: I am solid and dissolute. I write: my words are, like my sense of "I," both solid and dissolute. For every 100 times I am distracted, I come back 101 times to the apparently solid moments of everyday life to experience them fully as moments suffused with emptiness.

As an American Buddhist convert, the difficulties of this new convergence of West and East are exciting for me. In our small sanghas, or alone on our cushions, we are part of a larger hybrid religious culture in the United States. Part of my daily practice is to honor this hybridity as a writer—as someone simultaneously excited and beset by the solitary practice of the craft.

Five Verses for Shariputra Mugged Outside His Building

> *How can I expect a happy destiny*
> *If from my heart I summon*
> *Wandering beings to the highest bliss,*
> *But then deceive and let them down?*
> C Shantideva, *The Way of the Bodhisattva*

1.
Just a few car lengths from his front door
an old man stepped in Shariputra's way,
flat head curled, his pool-shark cap,
eyes gaping yellow and streaked with sizzled wires.
You'd think he didn't know Shariputra
just stepped out to mail a letter, actually a poem
to a woman he exchanged business cards with
on the train last week. She is broke,
dying a little with her savings every day.
In the poem Shariputra climbs
Mount Monadnock and looks across
tops of trees and sun setting
on New Hampshire and honestly believes
he cannot fall. "When I take a breath," he tells her,
"I am sure I will exhale. Why do I live each day
like I did on that mountain,
singularly sure I will not fall, though
evidence shows me the body is fragile,
docile, its perfect accomplishment dying?"

2.
Just these car lengths from home
the pool-shark man stepped in his way
and Shariputra walked around him.

Another man a block away yelled something
when Shariputra dropped the envelope
in the mailbox. Shariputra made a note:
this box is not picked up till four tomorrow.
He saw the shark-cap man with a woman

now laughing at the other man a block away
now running— and Shariputra regretted all this,
since he could wake early to mail this
tomorrow. Brighton Center's post office
picks up by nine in the morning.

3.
Now two car lengths from the mailbox
four college students who live above him
parallel parked their car and Shariputra
heard running increase behind him.
The man who was shouting kicked
Shariputra's feet, but he has vowed himself
an altruistic mind and managed not to fall.
The man was yelling and Shariputra
could not understand him, the words came
too fast, not even Sanskrit could save them.
The moon watched like a polished stone—
and as the man hit his face,
Shariputra knew the moonstone came
from underwater and his neighbors
probably were afraid to get out of their car.
Give me what you've got. Give me the wallet.
Shariputra handed it to him but touched it
first to his forehead—almost cost him his life.
The man snatched it from him too late:
Shariputra already blessed it, praying
credit cards could bring
this man good health, even bliss.

4.
But Shariputra lost his glasses, and this really is why the moon
took on its underwater luster. His cheek stung and something
swelled his face—with each heartbeat more swelling.

5.
Just a few car lengths from home,
his neighbors parallel parking,

and Shariputra thought he might die.
He could not see the man's lips move:
You got nothing here. No cash. Give me the cash
right now or you're a dead man.
But Shariputra had nothing, his glasses
were only made from plastic and he could not think
of anything else except his apartment keys.
He has no self and he said take this body—
you are so angry only this body can help.
The man kicked him to the ground and then
a few more times.
Shariputra gave up his vows then, saying
sentient beings are numberless and I
cannot help them because I never will know
what they wan—their desire is a mystery.
I think I am bleeding.
What are you going to do about it?
Shariputra got up, began walking away,
expected a knife in his back.
"Not a thing," he said. "No thing. I don't know."

Sitting, Wedding Morning

No birds in the window, just snow grains
curdled like gems on a tired tree.
Breathe out, this wind a trail of letters
we craned our necks to read across an ocean.
In, take back words at the start of a sigh —
no more separations, a postcard that always
makes its destination. Between each breath,
air so still outside you see violet.

The Body Is Fragile

A gull flicks down on a wave,
flies back against cutting wind into fog.

He clipped a speck between his claws,
an impossible fish, an inkspot pulled from the sea,

a new story, our memories cresting,
fresh mouths playing with our food.

Follow me back to a time when I didn't know
the body is fragile. Try to make it fresh,

like it's our first time over and over again.
I try to remember it for you,

the straight look of nothing special
about to happen, if you could remember

what the Cuyahoga looked like before it burned.
A whole city shuddered, scorched by its own river.

I recall, for you, my last breath before
the whoosh of baseball bat—that flash I remember,

too young to know why I couldn't exhale.
At tables around us, no one notices me

telling this story from so long ago,
when another kid smacked me with a bat

from behind, a gust of air that sent me
reeling. You taste a little garlic and anise

in the last knocky frames of free fall.
Sure, like your pasta plate right now,

this is how the brain abandons, strips you
for the two-bit thuggery and bare bulb

of the senses. That blow flared me, numb,
the field I fell rippled in front of me,

danced in blown branches. Everything went black,
but that's cliché and you say we can do better.

Old lovers, let's make it come alive—the napkins
on our laps, a wine bottle, the other tables snooping

for the bat crack—real groundswell and tide,
my young knees soft as tennis balls.

Chase Twichell

Biographical Sketch

Photo by Emma Dodge Hanson

Chase Twichell was born in 1950 and grew up in New Haven, Connecticut and the Adirondack Mountains of northern New York. She did her undergraduate work at Trinity College, and received an M.F.A. from the University of Iowa Writers' Workshop (1976). After working for a decade as a letterpress printer, typesetter, and book designer, she taught at Hampshire College, The University of Alabama, Goddard College, Warren Wilson College, and finally Princeton University (1990-1999). In 1999 she quit teaching to start Ausable Press, a not-for-profit independent literary press that publishes contemporary poetry.

Twichell has received fellowships from the National Endowment for the Arts, the New Jersey State Council on the Arts, and the John Simon Guggenheim Memorial Foundation, and a Literature Award from the American Academy of Arts and Letters. In 1997 she won the Alice Fay Di Castagnola Award from the Poetry Society of America for *The Snow Watcher*. She has published five volumes of poetry and a translation (with Tony K. Stewart) of Tagore. A new book, *Dog Language*, is forthcoming from Copper Canyon in 2005.

Living in the last significant wilderness east of the Rockies has been central to Twichell's life and work, as has her study of Buddhism. From 1995—2001 she was a student of John Daido Loori at Zen Mountain Monastery. She lives with her husband, novelist Russell Banks, in the Adirondacks.

Thoughts on Work and Zen

My practice of Zen began in earnest in 1994, when I was forty-four and found myself lacking for nothing in the world. I had good health, enough money to live comfortably, love, and the work of poetry. What more could there be? And yet, I was profoundly restless. In my work, I seemed to be inventing the world rather than living inside it. The making of a poem was for me a way to give a shape and a name to something ineffable, and thus come closer to its mystery, like trapping a wild animal in a flimsy cage long enough to take a look at it up close before it escaped again. I saw myself as a translator rendering the language of the world in English.

But what was this truth- and knowledge-seeking thing, this "self," this consciousness with a history and a memory, with passions and desires and hungers, joys and sufferings? Exactly what was it that was doing all this looking, interpreting, and recording? Heisenberg's Uncertainty Principle points out that the act of viewing changes the thing seen. He was talking about atomic particles, but it seems to me equally true of human consciousness. As I thought my way through the question of self—not *who* am I but *what* am I?—I saw what a strange fortress-like edifice I'd built, and decided to tear it down.

It was this effort that led me to Zen Mountain Monastery and John Daido Loori. Although I'm no longer formally a student there, the six years I spent trying to answer these questions changed my life and work profoundly. I hope that the poems show a consciousness more fully in the world, less defined by notions of self, and far, far, less of an authority about anything.

Rain in Ivy

I'm pondering the question
What hunts the leaf? No answer.
In the Monastery kitchen,
a dozen of us work in silence.
A koan is a monastery in your own head,
said Ta-hui, and as I set out to peel
a crate of acorn squash, I think he's right.
Rain makes the ivy move, as if
it were actively climbing.
It's metaphor to which my mind clings,
always too busy to see its own true nature.
I sharpen the knives just as my father
taught me, except here you don't spit
to wet the stone. I found the pocket knife
he lost, and hid it. I still have it.
I'm wondering where it is,
so when the drum sounds
marking the end of work time
I still don't know what hunts the leaf.

The All of It

I stood naked in the icy brook
under stars. I lay on hot granite
crisped with pearl-gray lichen
we crushed beneath us.

He tied trout flies with dog hair
and feathers, cooked the little fish
over the coals, on green sticks
he later burned, leaving nothing.

Was that it? Exactly that,
the Inside Knowledge,
the All of it?

Next and Last

Eating almonds and drinking
jasmine tea. Each almond
has its own fingerprint of flavor,
each sip of tea.
I'm unfaithful to both
the moment just passing
and the new one's
infant pain of sprouting,
the swelling gist
breaking the husk.
I'm a bee gathering gold-dust,
one of the winged seeds
spiraling through November's
ochre under-things,
a moving target,
reflex, spasm, distraction,
sun behind a cloud—
two moments not even strung,
the passing and the new,
but blown for a nanosecond
by the same wind.

Faraway leaves haunt the tea,
also kid voices barely there and not
for long, so if I want to hear their
last words I have to commit
to hearing them right here, right now.
Or the pot cools,
and the ghosts go away forever.

The Quality of Striving

Eye-catching as a dog on a chain,
tough-muscled, brash,
talking fifty-fifty words/harmonica,
Bob Dylan let himself as an old man
sit in on the songs.
I want words half zendo,
half casino, like his,
cruder and more fluent than this,
with a swelling inevitability about them,
an itch, the way a bud must itch
before it breaks.

If you think northern spring
is more beautiful than spring in the south,
then on some level you understand
that I write by the light of the secret
Protestant pride in asceticism,
the most seductive Buddha of all.

My war pits sleep's enthrallments
against those of consciousness.
I often encounter a miniature
localized tiredness,
droopy yellow flag marking
a tree to come down.
Next second I'm setting out to master
the subspecies of all conifers in the region
and the first five hundred
Latin vocabulary flashcards.

It's late again, and I'm tired,
too tired to take up the great
work of introspection,
to be a spur to myself.
But what drives me

to be a spur?
Why not a lullaby sung
in the hammock's hinge-screak,
sound of the word *squander?*
What hungry ghost in me
rises and strips off
the self-scented sheets before dawn?

Soul in Space

How did it come to be
that a particular human loneliness
set forth into clouds of ignorance
so as to more closely examine itself?
Why one, and so few others?

I stand among shoulder-high canes,
looking directly into their barbed
inner dark to the snake, or caterpillar—
actually a handful of blackberries
in the green shade, reptilian
yet warm, momentarily still.

I want my obituary to say that
I wrote in the language of dogs,
and not that I sat sprinkling
black letters on a white ladder,
leading my own eye down
one rung at a time
until the dog was gone.

Photo by Kai Sibley

Anne Waldman

Biographical Sketch

Born April 2, 1945 in Millville, New Jersey, Anne Waldman became part of the late Sixties poetry scene in the New York's East Village. She ran the St. Mark's Church Poetry Project, where she gave exuberant physical readings of her own work.

"She became a Buddhist, worshipping with the Tibetan Chogyam Trungpa Rinpoche, who would also become Allen Ginsberg's guru. She and Ginsberg worked together to create a poetry school, the Jack Kerouac School of Disembodied Poetics, at Trungpa's Naropa Institute in Boulder, Colorado.

Waldman is one of the post-Beat poetry community. "Her confluence of Buddhist concerns and thought-paths with sources of physicality and anger is particularly impressive. Over the years, she has worked her magic on audiences throughout the United States and around the world, giving poetry readings in Germany, England, Italy, Scotland, Czechoslovakia, Norway, The Netherlands, Bali, India, Nicaragua and Canada. She has also worked and performed with a number of well-known musicians, composers and dancers. More recently, she has collaborated with many visual artists."

She has written more than 42 books, most recently *In the Room of Never Grieve: New and Selected Poems* (Coffee House Press 2003), *Kill or Cure* (Penguin Poets) and her book-length poem, *Iovis* (Coffee House Press). "A major voice in American poetry, she delves deeply into the masculine soul and its sources of energy. Her goal is to speak against, about, around and through the all-pervasive forces of Western patriarchy and its many manifestations."

Zen Statement:

In effect, what I'm attempting to do on the page is to give readers not 'a refined gist' or 'an extrapolation' of feeling, thought and emotion, but an actual experience of a high moment. I want to bring to poetry on the page the same kind of immediacy and sense of immersion one can bring in public performance.

(from *The Museum of Modern Poetics*;
http://www.poetspath.com/waldman.html)

Recalling Former Travels

for Philip Whalen, after Tu Mu

lolled in
  meditation halls
bowed down to temple ground

gong it struck thus:

vernalization?

  keep talking about seeds

enlightenment DNA

or the vernix of mind

        blasphemy for the turncoat world
& what gets quelled

  my waist my head my feet disappeared
in obeisance to mind

what is "little mind"?

drollery...
    linguistics...
  respite from the very next thing...

  or mind is the very next thing

  rung on a ladder
a tongue a wag of which moves you
  to stop

reels of talk

stop the queue of mind
    all lines being mind are minded here

then glimmer
    (blue eye)

old memory: lantern
the night he arrived for steak dinner
    & it got burnt

phalansterian he might be

& never misread the body politic

on the lookout mountain

                        mind went over the mountain
or mind jumped in the wooden cart

        prefer a synoptic account?

mind sat in a thousand places
drinking tea
writing thus as notation
of all that silken mind weaves

        segments meant to swim

black silk like smooth *naga* skin
red silk that takes your breath away
        like seduction
yellow silk for Thailand

the silk road entered mind
mind entered civilization

when you walk you are not a rock
rock could be the corner of a tomb-civilization

mind, at least a bit of it, went into ink
ink came from mineral rock
went into branch

you stood gaping over the femur et cetera

awareness, perception, refusing, judgement

you stood drooling over the *bon mot* et cetera

awareness, morphology, steel-cage-frivolity

did you?

Japan: was it strict?

the sensible horizon
like an Horatian ode would never be
sung

tricking you
& come as conqueror to the point of an anvil
electromagnetic fields to a point of despair

can't hold all this in my mind

larynx larynx dear Philip
walking the prodigy world

    a mountain for your thought

glad we stuck together

wasted no time
       climbed dharma rope
     obscure being mind
   hills

making the poetry tree musculature

hills being mind wasted no time climbing

obscured

being mind inside the obscuring mind

WAKE UP
or

salt the wound again

WAKE UP

it is possible to mind the mind

saw the mountainw orld
wind around us

    Himalays
      Andes
        Rockies

gave up being mind

or never minded giving up the mind

to you

bow many times

on hallucinatory "bank and shoal of time"

Admonitions of the Boudoir
-after *Meng Chiao (751-814 B.C.E)*

keep away from sharp words
don't go near a beautiful woman
barbed semantics such as "missile" "debt" "ownership"
"depression" "cleansed" "torrential flood"
  wound your *logopoeia*

woman's beauty up close-gold tooth
  wrinkled brow
  quixotic smile
  a wit to vie with?
upsets desire

cancel assignations of a perigee moon!

dangers of the highway are not about distance either
  or speed limits whatever vehicle you drive

danger of passion is not in loving too often
one hour with you, scarred for life

In the Room of Never Grieve

register
& escape
  the traps

a last judgment

cheetah under her skin

one window on the sunny side

still life with stylus

w/ rancor
still life w/ daggers
size of a postcard

no harm will come to the dolls
which I am the queen

ghosts gather—
scald
seethe

One Inch of Love Is an Inch of Ashes

Allen Ginsberg came to me in a dream:

> *it's goofy here,*
> *all the conversations are in my head*
> *the gods & goddesses get busy*
> *(commune) with the world, day in day out*
> *they're distracted*
> *I have no body! No notebooks*
> *I'm scribing my good looks & dangerous poetry*
> *on heaven*
> *Heaven's so BIG too, & there's lots of rogues*
> *around*
> *I'm just a Nobody*
>
> *You know what the Chinese poet said, Anne,*
> *"one inch of love is an inch of ashes."*

Some Other American Zen Poets
with Recent Works

L.N. Allen (Nicola, CT) has published in *Long Island Quarterly*.

Frank Anthony (Windsor, VT) has published in *The Anthology of New England Writers*.

Lucy Aron (Sebastopol, CA) has published in *Nimrod International Journal* and *Peregine*.

Dick Bakken (Bisbee, AZ) *12 Greatest Hits* (Pudding House).

Deborah Bogen (Pittsburgh, PA) grew up in the 1960s in Marin County, CA.

Sharon Baker (Findlay, OH) is a Midwest poet.

Guy R. Beining (Lee, MA) has published six books of poetry and 25 chapbooks.

Patrick Blessinger (Marietta, OH) teaches at Georgia Perimeter College.

Katherine Blackbird (Barton, OH) CD *A Year Without God; White Sustenance* (KSU Press).

Doug Bolling (Jacksonville, IL) has edited *Par Rapport* and his poetry has appeared in *Mid-America Poetry Review*.

John Bradley (DeKalb, IL) is the editor of *Learning to Glow: A Nuclear Reader* ; *Terrestrial Music* (Curbstone Press).

Christopher Buckley (Lompoc, CA) *Sky* (Sheep Meadow Press).

Robin Chapman (Madison, WI) *The Way In* (Tebot Bach).

Margaret Chula (Portland, OR) edits Katsura Press; *Shadow Lines*.

Deborah Crooks (San Francisco, CA) has published in *The Sun*.

Todd Davis (Altoona, PA) teaches at Penn State Altoona; *Ripe: Poems* (Bottom Dog Press).

Jeanne Desy (Columbus, OH) leads poetry workshops; *Cat! The Animal that Hides in Your Heart* (Ingle Nook Press).

CX Dillhunt (Madison, WI) *Girl Saints* (Fireweed Press).

Susan Elbe (Madison, WI) *Light made from Nothing* (Parallel Press).

Karl Elder (Sheboygan, WI) teaches at Lakeland Colleg; *A Man of Pieces* (Prickly Pear Press).

Lawrence Forbes (Cleveland, OH) shares his poems in the Midwest.

Gary Gach (San Francisco, CA) *The Complete Idiot's Guide to Understanding Buddhism*.

Joshua Gage (Pepper Pike, OH) is an editor for *Whisky Island Review* and at Hedgehog Press.

Lorence A. Gutterman (Columbus, OH) is a retired medical oncologist and poet.

Coco Gordon (New York, NY) is publisher of Water Mark Press and an intermedia artist.

Peggy Heinrich (Bridgeport, CT) *Sharing the Woods* (Old Sandal Press).

Joy Harold Helsing (Magalia, CA) *Waiting for Winter* (Poet's Corner Press).

Ailish Hopper (Baltimore, MD) teaches at Goucher College and has appeared in *Poetry Kanto.*

Joy St. John Johnson (Huntsville, AL) has been influenced by Allen Watts.

M.J. Iuppa (Hamlin, NY) *Night Traveler* (Foothills Publishing).

Susan Kelly-DeWitt (Sacramento, CA) has published in *Poetry* and *Prairie Schooner.*

Julie Kane (Natchitoches, LA) teaches at Northwestern State University and has published in *The Southern Review* and *The Taos Review.*

R.Kimm (Marcellus, NY) has published hundreds of poems.

Tom Koontz (Selma, IN) has published widely.

Michael Kriesec (Aniwa, WI) has worked as a journalist and published in *Chinese Review* and *Plainsongs.*

Jill J. Lange (Cleveland Hts., OH) has published in *Tributaries.*

Jeanne Larsen (Roanoke, VA) is a writer of Buddhist novels and poetry.

Mark Lamoureux (Allston, MA) is editor of *Fulcrum Annual; 29 Cheeseburgers* (Pressed Wafer).

Charlene Langfur (Waldwick, NJ) teaches at William Patterson University and has published in *The Adirondack Review.*

Cathy Lentes (Middleport, OH) is an award winning poet and has published in several new anthologies.

Chad Lietz (Las Vegas, NV) edits for *Interim, Red Rock Review* and *Mamaliga.*

Harvey Lillywhite (Baltimore, MD) received an NEA Artist Grant for Poetry.

Melissa Marconi (Santa Clara, CA) teaches at San Jose State and Santa Clara Universities and has published in *Two Girls Review.*

David B. McCory (Massillon, OH) *The Geometry of Blue* and *Buffalo Time.*

Jack McGuane (Lakewood, OH) is retired from production work and now enjoys writing poetry.

Patricia Monaghan (Chicago, IL) *Dancing with Chaos* (Salmon Poetry) and *Meditation: The Complete Guide* with Eleanor Vierick.

Joesph McLaughlin (Dover, OH) is a retired professor from Stark College of Technology; *Greatest Hits* (Pudding House).

Christopher Meyer (Danville, OH) *Twenty-eight Pages Lovingly Bond with Twine.*

J.D. Mitchell (Las Vegas, NV) edits for *Red Rock Review* and *Cricket Online Review*.

E. Ethelbert Miller (Washington, DC) *Buddha Weeping in Winter* (Red Dragon Press).

Leslea' Newman (Northampton, MA) *Still Life with Buddha: a novel told in fifty poems* (Windstorm Creative).

John Nizalowski (Grand Junction, CO) *Hooking the Sun* (Farolito Press).

Natalie Palmieri (Cleveland, OH) is a Midwest poet.

James Penha (Jakarta, Indonesia) a native New Yorker, teaches at the Jakarta International School.

Geoffrey Philip (N. Miami Beach, FL) is a Caribbean writer; author of the novel *Benjamin, My Son* and four collections of poetry.

Lynn Porcello (South Euclid, OH) is a member of "Night Vision," a women's writing group.

Kenneth Pobo (Folsom, PA) teaches at Widener University and has published in *Nimrod* and *Heartlands*.

Deborah Poe (Bellingham, WA) is in the graduate program at Western Washington University.

Kakashezi P. (Tempe, AZ) a native of Japan now residing in America.

Susan Azar Porterfield (DeKelb, IL) teaches at Rockford College and is the editor of *Zen, Poetry, the Art of Lucian Stryk* (Ohio Univ. Press).

David Radavich (Charleston, IL) *By the Way: Poems over the Years* (Buttonwood Press).

Tom Rechtin (Binghamton, NY) is in the graduate program at Binghamton University.

Susan Rich (Seattle, WA) award- winning *The Cartographer's Tongue/ Poems of the World*.

Susanna Rich (Blairstown, NJ) teaches at Kean University and is a Fulbright Scholar working on her memoir.

Charles P. Ries (Milwaukee, WI) *Monje Malo Speaks English* (Lockout Press).

J.E. Robinson (Alton, IL) has published in *Mid-America Poetry Review*

Linda Goodman Robiner (Cleveland, OH) has taught at John Carroll University; *Reverse Fairy Tale* (Pudding House).

Kate Robinson (Chino Valley, AZ) has published in literacy journals and anthologies.

Michael Rothenberg (Miami, FL) has studied with and edited the work of Joanne Kyger and Philip Whalen; *Unhurried Visions* (La Alameda Press).

Charles Rossiter (Oak Park, IL) *Cold Mountain 2000: Han-Shan in the City* (Backwoods Broadsides).

Peter Seidman (Berkeley, CA) works with blending Kaballah, Buddhism, and Taoism.

Joanne Seltzer (Schenectady, NY) has published in numerous journals and anthologies.

Penny Skillman (San Francisco, CA) *The Cat's Journal* and has recently completed *Californio Meditates.*

Hal Sirowitz (Brooklyn, NY) is the Former Poet Laureate of Queens, NY; *Father Said* (Soft Skull Press).

Joseph Somoza (Las Cruces, NM) *Cityzen* (La Alameda Press).

Jeanine Stevens (Sacramento, CA) has published poetry in *Tiger's Eye* and widely with other journal and anthologies.

Jody Stewart (Hawley, MA)

Carl Stilwell (Pasadena, CA) has published in *Struggle* and *Blue Collar Review.*

Elaine Terranova (Philadelphia, PA) *The Dog's Heart* (Orchises Press) and *The Cult of the Right Hand* (Doubleday).

Mark Thalman (Forest Grove, OR) has published in journals and anthologies.

Richard Thomas (Las Cruces, NM) taught at Michigan State University; *Frog Praises Night* (Southern Ill. Univ. Press).

J.A. Vanek (Oberlin, OH) is a physician and poet whose writings have appeared in literary journals.

Michael Waldecki (Lorain, OH) *Crown of Creation* (Black Oak Press).

Michael Waters (Salisbury, MD) has published poetry widely.

Steve Wilson (San Marcos, TX) was a Fulbright Scholar in Maribor, Slovenia and his poems have been widely published in journals and anthologies.

Andrena Zawinski (Oakland, CA) is Features Editor for <*Poetry Magazine. com.*

Partial Acknowledgements

"The Dead Do Not Want Us Dead," © 2001 Jane Hirshfield; first appeared in *Tricycle: The Buddhist Review*; reprinted in *Poets Against The War*, edited by Sam Hamill (NY: Nation Books, 2003. Used by permission of Jane Hirshfield.

"The Monk Stood Beside the Wheelbarrow," © 2002 Jane Hirshfield; first appeared in *The Shambhala Sun*. Used by permission of JaneHirshfield.

"To Judgement: An Assay," © 2003 Jane Hirshfield; first appeared in *Poetry*. Used by permission of Jane Hirshfield.

"It Was Like This: You Were Happy," © 2002 Jane Hirshfield; first appeared in *The New Yorker*. Used by permission of Jane Hirshfield.

"Lights Out" by John Gilgun appeared previously in *The New-Victorian/ Cochlea*, Vol.One, Number Two, Fall-Winter 2002-2003 (Madison, WI).

Anne Waldman's poems from *In the Room of Never Grieve: New and Selected Poems 1985-2003* appear with permission from the author and Coffee House Press © 2003.

Margaret Gibson's poems appear with permission of the author and Louisiana State University Press. *Icon and Evidence: Poems* by Margaret Gibson © 2001 by Margaret Gibson and *Grasses: Poems* by Margaret Gibson © 2003 by Margaret Gibson.

Lines from Gary Snyder's poem "Axe Handles" from *Axe Handles: Poems* by Gary Snyder © 1983 North Point Press.

"Preface" Craig Paulenich and Kent Johnson, eds, "Introduction" by Gary Snyder. *Beneath a Single Moon: Buddhism in Contemporary American Poetry* (Boston: Shambhala Publications 1991).

Our Artists

Lois Eby grew up in Tulsa, Oklahoma, with summer trips to the islands of Ontario, Canada. Dreams together with reflection on energy, life and art have led her painting into the improvisational and abstract. She lives with poet David Budbill in northern Vermont where her art is exhibited. See her webpage at: **http://www.loiseby.com/**

George Fitzpatrick

"George Fitzpatrick's work is a kind of calligraphy that weds meticulous presentation of words and pattern with a musical, rhythmic approach to the development of their formal properties across a sheet of paper. He developed this idiom in 1974." -Carter E. Foster

George Fitzpatrick is a Cleveland artist, and his work is handled by Salander-O'Reily of New York. He has done a series of works tied to Cold Mountain, Tu Fu, Su Tung P'o, and other Chinese Zen poets.

Air Conditioned Buddha, shop window, Woodstock, New York,
photo by Larry Smith